GEMS FROM

GENESIS

BIBLE STUDY AIDS *of William G. Heslop*

*Gems From Genesis
*Extras From Exodus
*Lessons From Leviticus
*Nuggets From Numbers
*Rubies From Ruth
*Sermon Seeds From The Psalms
*Pearls From the Poets and Prophets
*Diamonds From Daniel

GEMS FROM GENESIS

An Outlined Study

by
William G. Heslop, D.D., Litt., S.D.

KREGEL PUBLICATIONS
Grand Rapids, Michigan 49501

Library of Congress Catalog Card Number: 75-13661
ISBN 0-8254-2825-4

First edition 1940
Kregel Publications edition . . 1975
Reprinted 1979, 1983

Printed in the United States of America

CONTENTS

GENESIS

Twofold Division

Enlighten your study of New Testament
with these basic gems of truth.

"Even a casual study of religions and the effects of religions in the lives of people makes one fact very evident, namely, that one's conception of God is the one supreme factor in molding his thinking, his conceptions, his conclusions, his ethics, his morals, in fact, every phase of his life. Everything depends, in the final analysis, upon one's conception of God. This is basic, it is elemental, around it everything revolves. Here lies the chief trouble with all religions aside from the religion of our Lord Jesus Christ, including Hinduism, Islam, Buddhism and all others."

Dr. R. T. Williams

(Glimpses Abroad, p. 125)

1

THE FIRST EARTH

"In the beginning God created the heavens and the earth"—Gen. 1:1.

We wish you to think back before the time when you were born, *back* before your parents were born, *back* before your grandparents were born, *back* before the birth of Abraham Lincoln or George Washington, *back* before the conversion of Peter, back before the conversion of Paul, *back* before the birth of Christ, *back* before any prophets uttered a single prophecy, *back* before the reigns of Solomon or David, *back* before the days of Samuel or the times of the Judges, *back* before Joshua led God's people into Canaan, *back* before Moses led them out of Egypt, *back* before Abram left Ur of Chaldees, *back* before Noah entered the ark, *back* before Cain murdered his own brother, *back* before the creation and fall of our first parents in Eden, *back* before there was an Eden in which they could be created, *back* before there was a place called earth for them to inherit, *back* before there was either an angel or archangel, *back* before a sun, moon, or star shone in the heaven, *back* six thousand years, *back* six million years, *back,* as far back as your mind can travel, *back* into the eternity past when there was only ONE GOD in three persons, *back* when there was only One God oc-ᵣcupying the stage, *back* into the eternity past when God, the Father, and God, the Holy Ghost, and God, the Son occupied the arena of the universes.

In sacred council assembled, the Trinity met and decided that they would create flaming worlds. No sooner was it decided than it was done and from the tips of omnipotent fingers there swung into space millions of flaming suns, multiplied thousands of light bearing moons, and innumerable companies of scintillating stars. Once again the sacred council met and decided that they would make flaming spirits some of whom would occupy some of those flaming worlds. No sooner was it decided than it was done, the Word was spoken and there came into being millions of burning, shining, flaming spirits, angels and archangels, morning stars and sons of the morning, cherubim and seraphim, with Michael and Gabriel and Lucifer as their chiefs, heads, or generalissimos. These millions of bright cherubic and seraphic spirit intelligences were each and all individually created by God. The angelic hosts have not come from one holy pair as did the human family. They were created endless, undying spirits and created individually by the divine Word. Lucifer was the principal or chief of the angelic hosts called morning stars or sons of the dawning. He and they heralded the coming of a glorious day. They were amongst the beginnings of the angelic millions. Gabriel and Michael were also chiefs of other of the spirit luminosities. There are various orders of the angelic multitude with various degrees of honor, glory, majesty, dignity and power, and they were each and all individually and personally created by God. There are no family relationships among the angels. These angelic beings filled various offices in the ordered government of God. They knew themselves to be endless undying spirits and perfectly understood that their eternal happiness and well-being depended upon their allegiance and obedience to the Creator. With flaming shining wings and luminous spirit bodies they could speed through space at the rate of light and they were the beginnings of God's wonderful creation in His wonderful ordered universe.

Again, the sacred three met together and decided that they would make one more world. Again, it was no sooner decided than it was done and from the little finger tip of Omnipotence there swung into space the world which we now know as the earth. A world so beautiful, a world so wonderful, a world so glorious and magnificent that when it swung into space the Morning Stars sang together and the Sons of God shouted for joy. This beautiful earth with its transparent atmosphere called the heavens was so luminous and beautiful that the choir lofts of the angelic world rang with their jubilant shouts and songs of praise to the wonderful Creator. "In the beginning God created the heavens and the earth."

IN THE BEGINNING. *Not* six thousand years ago, not seven thousand years ago, or seventy thousand years ago, but in the beginning. As far back as your mind can travel, *in the beginning*.

IN THE BEGINNING GOD. Here is where we all must begin. If we fail to begin here we shall spend our days, years and life with a guess and reckon and perhaps and probably and it is likely and it seems to me and it is my opinion. One man's opinion is as good as that of another. One person's guess is as good as that of another. The guesses of a Professor Barnes or the ravings of an Ingersol or the learned probabilities of a Fosdick or Eddy or Brisbane cannot satisfy the human heart or mind. We are a lot of imbeciles and derelicts unless we begin where the Bible begins, *In the begin-*

ning God. The Bible makes no attempt to prove that there is a God. If the Bible had been conceived in the brain of man and written by the pen of man, he would have immediately set out to prove the existence of God. No such attempt is ever made in the Bible and right here is our first proof that the Bible is God's Book. The Bible begins with God, and a man is a fool unless he begins with God.

In the beginning God CREATED. Not evolved. Not by a long gradual process. Not through millions of years of struggle, but in the beginning God CREATED. The Word of God begins with creation. It is impossible to be a Bible Christian and a modern evolutionist at the same time. A modern evolutionist is not a Christian. *In the beginning God created* cannot possibly be pulled and twisted to mean evolved. Modern evolution is a result of the imbecile ravings of Godless brains. We must begin with GOD and begin with CREATION or we shall end as unmitigated fools notwithstanding the fact that we may have graduated from seven schools, colleges, and universities.

In the beginning God created THE HEAVENS. There are three heavens plainly revealed in the Bible. The first heaven is the atmosphere which surrounds our earth, revolves with the earth and is a part of the earth. The second heaven is the starry heavens with its millions of suns, moons and stars. The third heaven is the home of God and the center of all life and light. In the beginning God created the heavens.

In the beginning God created the heavens AND THE EARTH. This first verse of the Bible sounds the death knell of evolution. "In the beginning God created the EARTH." This was in the eternity of ages past.

That the Creation account is unscientific and in clash with the discoveries of modern science is one of the common statements. It has, however, no foundation whatever. The proofs that there is no error in the account of Creation as revealed in the first chapter of Genesis, have been furnished by the investigation of Science. The order of creation as given in the first chapter is the order, which, after years of searching—the most laborious searching—Science has discovered. Over and over again has Science with its guesses and speculations been forced to bow in submission before the simple and brief description of the Creation in God's Word. There is no clash between the Bible and the results of true scientific research. Geology, astronomy and other sciences have had to retrace their steps more than once and acknowledge their mistake; the first chapter of Genesis will never have to do that."

A. C. Gaebelein
(The Annotated Bible, Vol 1)

2

THE FIRST CATACLYSM

"The earth was without form and void and darkness was upon the face of the deep." Genesis 1:2

Think back far enough until you reach the eternity that is past. Elohim had created the heavens and the earth. God created all things good and to be inhabited. There was no waste and no darkness and no sin and no disorder and nothing void. The Holy Trinity in council assembled decided that over the beautiful and perfect earth they would anoint Lucifer as the first king, president, governor or ruler. Lucifer, who was the chief of the Sons of the Morning, was placed over the fair and wondrous and luminous earth and annointed to be the Cherub who should rule this kingdom and empire for God. Under this flaming cherub there were an innumerable host of angelic beings. Lucifer, THE Son of the Morning, the anointed cherub, full of wisdom, perfect in beauty, and with every precious stone as his covering, walking up and down in the midst of the stones of fire, perfect in his ways from the day of his creation, the brightest and most excellent and honorable of all the angelic hosts, was placed over the beautiful freshly created Earth and became its king and lord.

At stated intervals he ascended and appeared before the Supreme Majesty in the Heaven of Heavens to render an account of his kingdom and doings, for all creatures whether angelic or human must render an account to God.

While rendering an account of his empire and reporting the state of all his dominions and the condition of all the subordinates in his empire, he noticed ONE PERSON greater than he; one person who was more glorious than he; one person with more dignity, honor and majesty than he; one person more luminous and wonderful than himself. The sight of that ONE person in the Heaven of Heavens presented to Lucifer the temptation to seek that place, position and power. The outward temptation became an inward desire, his heart was lifted up with pride, and he determined in his heart to ascend into heaven and exalt his throne above the stars of God, sit upon the mount of the congregation, go up above the heights of the clouds, *and be like the MOST HIGH*. He decided and determined in his heart that he would go up and usurp the place and position of Christ. He determined to be like the Most High. The expression "The Most High" is one of the names of our Lord Jesus Christ. No sooner did he decide and determine to exalt himself than he began a whispering campaign among his subordinate angels and one-third of the angels under him rallied to his support. His luminous feet lifted from the earth and he sped away through the heavens. When he reached the limit of his empire, which is the Aerial Spaces, a judgment stroke from Omnipotence fell upon him, and he became the black winged monster of iniquity whom we now know as the devil or Satan. He fell to the earth like lightning and the once perfect, shining Lucifer became the prince of the power of the air and the arch-enemy of Christ. Not only was Lucifer stricken with divine judgment because of his rebellion, but his empire and kingdom, THE EARTH with its ATMOSPHERE, was also smitten by the judgments of God. The earth was smitten; the mountains were turned upside down; the rocks were turned inside out and a thousand volcanoes spued out liquid fire. Black smoke-clouds put out the light of the sun and the earth staggered to and fro and rocked and reeled like a drunken man. The beautiful earth became a waste and void and God Almighty wrapped a dense impenetrable mantle of darkness around the globe.

Gen. 1:1—In the beginning God created the heavens and the earth.

Gen. 1:2—The earth was without form and void and darkness upon the face of the deep.

Gen. 1:1 describes the original creation.

Gen. 1:2 describes the first dreadful cataclysm.

Darkness and waste and chaos are always the result of sin. This was in the Eternity past. The problem of sin was thus on God's hands long before the race was created in the Garden of Eden!

Without the Bible we know nothing of the past eternity and without the Bible we know nothing of the future.

The Creation

I. The Fact of the Creation

    1. Genesis is the book of beginnings. It sets forth the beginnings of the heavens, the earth, sin, darkness, man, marriage, salvation, punishment, the sabbath, sonship, service and sacrifice. It describes the beginning of the Human Race through Adam . . . . the Chosen Race through Shem and Abraham . . . the Colored Race through Ham . . . . and the White Race through Japheth.

       It is the Seed plot of the Bible. Every fundamental doctrine of Christianity is to be found in Genesis.

2. Genesis gives the only authentic account of Creation. It is so simple and yet so full and sublime that it cannot possibly be improved.

3. Genesis 1:1 is the only original, full, complete, true account of Creation. Genesis 1:3 to the end is dealing with RESTORATION and NOT with CREATION. In the beginning God created the earth. He created it good, orderly, not a waste, chaos, void. He created it out of nothing and created it to be inhabited. The Prophets Jeremiah and Isaiah and Ezekiel clearly indicate that the earth had undergone a catastrophic change as the result of the sin and rebellion of angels and the consequent judgments of God. The earth bears the marks of such a cataclysmic upheaval.

Read carefully and prayerfully the following Scriptures:

Jer. 4:23-26
Isa. 14:9-14
Isa. 24:1
Isa. 45:18
Ezek. 28:12-15

4. The Word *God* in Genesis 1:1 in the Hebrew is ELOHIM. The Hebrew word EL means "the strong one, the almighty" and Elohim is the plural for God as Cherubim is the plural for Cherub and Seraphim is the plural for Seraph and thus we have a revelation of the Trinity in Genesis 1:1.

5. The word *created* means to bring into existence without any pre-existing material from which

to make them. It means to bring something out of nothing.

6. Creation was in the eternity past before time or day and night began. The six days work of Genesis 1 was not created but restoration.
It did not take God six days to create. He created in the beginning. It took six days to restore the earth to its original condition and then climax the restoration by the creation of man.
The Creation of the Earth was before time began. Genesis 1:1.
The time element of day and night entered in its restoration and not in its creation.

7. The seven days of Genesis 1 were literal days NOT of creation, but of restoration and climaxing the restoration by placing man upon the earth.
All the ages required by Science are in the first verse. "In the beginning God created . . . the earth" NOT six thousand (6,000) years ago, but in the beginning.
The number seven is a significant number. It is the number of perfection. Seven days in the week.
Seven years comprise the cycle of Jewish years.
Seven spirits of God denote the Holy Spirit.
Seven Candlesticks set forth the Church.
Seven stars refer to the ministers of the seven churches.
Enoch was the Seventh (7) from Adam.
Enoch translated that he should not see death before the judgment of the flood is a type of

the bridehood saints who shall be translated when the Lord Jesus comes *for* his saints and before the great tribulation floods of Divine Wrath sweep the earth. Japheth begat seven sons and these constitute the White Gentile Nations of the earth.

It is more than likely that there will be seven thousand years history of Man. The Millennium will probably be the seventh thousand years.

8. Genesis 1 is typical throughout. It speaks of the New Birth, the New Creation where all was chaos and ruin, and on the seventh day God rested. It is more than likely that God's Millennial rest will be the seventh Day or seventh thousand years of the history of Man.

The word "day" has several usages in Scripture:

1. A period of twenty-four hours.

2. Something distinctive as "day of Atonement."

3. A period of time which may be long or short as "day of judgment."

4. An age or dispensation as "day of Salvation," "Man's day," and "day of the Lord."

Today is the "day of Salvation."

Today is also "Man's day."

Tomorrow may be the "day of the Lord," "the day of God," and the "day of judgment."

The exact meaning of the word "day" must be

decided by the context and comparing scripture with scripture.

9. Genesis is quoted more than sixty times in the New Testament and in seventeen books of the New Testament.

10. All subsequent revelation is planted deeply in the soil of Genesis and without Genesis we would be ignorant of the early history of the world or man.

11. Grass and fruit. It is not necessary to suppose that the life germ of all seeds perished in the judgments of Genesis 1:2. When light was spoken into the darkness of the ruined earth now restored, the earth would bring forth as described in verse 11.

12. Sun and Moon. The two great lights mentioned in verses 14-16 were made to appear and NOT create on the fourth day. A different word is used which does not imply an original creative act as in verse 1. The Sun and Moon of verse 16 were made visible or made to appear, having already been created in verse 1.

"The Holy Spirit is not imparted to men as a deposit to be jealously guarded and economically used—He comes at once as an in-filling and out-flowing Spirit. Like Pison, Gihon, Hiddekel and Euphrates, streams which emerged from the river in Eden, so the Holy Spirit proceeding from the Father and the Son breaks into manifold channels as it flows through the lives of men. In the light of this symbol, how significant are the meanings of these words. Pison means 'overflowing'; Gihon, 'breaking forth'; Hiddegel, 'velocity'; and Euphrates, 'sweet waters'.

"Men heed not only an inward spring of life for their own salvation, they need the overflow for the salvation of others. If sanctification puts rivers of living water into the soul, then one of the evidences of sanctification should be rivers of living water flowing out from the soul. The Holy Ghost as the gift of the glorified Christ, purifies the hearts of men, and so fills them with His presence that the gladdening streams flow out for the strengthening of others. There is a river, the streams whereof shall make glad the city of God."

Dr. H. Orton Wiley.

3

THE DOVE-LIKE SPIRIT

"And the Spirit of God moved upon the face of the waters." Genesis 1:2.

In the Eternity that is past, God created the heaven and the earth and all the angelic hosts. In the eternity past Lucifer fell from his high and holy position and became Satan or the Devil. The earth with its atmosphere suffered by the judgments of God as a consequence of the sin of Lucifer. The earth was wrapped in thick darkness. Crepe was put on the door-knob of a world. All this was in the eternity that is past. Once again the Divine Trinity met and decided that they would restore the heavens and earth. The third person of the blessed Trinity descended upon the darkness and ruin and brooded and moved upon it as a dove brooding over and upon its eggs. The creation, the sin and fall of angels, judgment upon the earth, chaos, waste, and darkness, together with the mission of the Holy Spirit to restore the ruined creation, was all in the Eternity past before day or night or time commenced. Selah!

"In the beginning God created the heavens and the earth, and the earth was without form and void and darkness was upon the face of the deep *and the Spirit of God moved upon the face of the waters.*"

The Holy Spirit has always been the active agent and executive of the God-head. He brooded over the darkness of a ruined world. He was the sword of flame Who kept the first sinners away from the tree of life.

He was pictured to us in the thrilling story of Eliezer who was sent to obtain a bride for the loving Father's obedient son, Isaac. He was pictured to us again in the story of Joseph's steward who brought the brethren of Joseph to see their true condition and realize their awful wickedness in their rejection of Joseph. He was typified by the oil in the candlestick in the ancient tabernacle and also by the pillar of fire, the water out of the rock, the rushing wind and the gentle dew. He was also pen-pictured to us in the thrilling histories of Joshua and Elisha, as well as in the master-workman and engraver Bezaleel. *The still small voice* heard in I Kings 19 also sets forth the gentle ministry of the Spirit.

The Spirit of God began His ministry in Eternity past. His presence and power was felt and manifested throughout the Old Testament. In the days of the Judges the Holy Spirit moved the deliverers or saviors or so-called judges. Even in the case of the enigmatic and paradoxical Samson, the Holy Spirit moved him betimes in the camp of Dan. The strength of Samson was not in his head, nor in his arm, nor in his hair, but in the Holy Ghost. Down through the centuries the Holy Spirit moved and worked until at last He descended on the Holy Christ. It was the Holy Spirit Who pressed Jesus on towards His conflict with Satan in the wilderness. It was through the power of the Spirit that Jesus performed His stupendous miracles.

Quickened by the Spirit He arose from the dead. Quickened by the Spirit He preached to the spirits in prison. The day of Pentecost arrived and the Holy Ghost descended in purity and power upon the apostolic band and the dispensation of the Spirit was ushered in. As the seven fold Spirit, He will operate during the great tribulation, and, during the millennium, He will be the Chief Detective in the righteous government of God.

There are many figurative representations used in the Bible to set forth the work of the Holy Spirit. These emblems of the Holy Spirit set for some very special phases of the Spirit's work.

1. *Rain* sets forth the abundance and grace of the Spirit's supply. It also is a minister of judgment to the ungodly. The Rain is a bringer of blessing. It comes at stated seasons and intervals and is very refreshing and plentiful. It may also be a minister of judgment. The Holy Spirit may be quenched, grieved, insulted.

2. *Wind* sets forth the mysterious, but none the less effective operation of the Holy Spirit. It is invisible, mysterious, powerful, cleansing, purifying, mighty and rushing. Wind also may be an agent of destruction and death. The Holy Spirit may depart and leave the soul beyond that line by us unseen which crosses every path, the hidden boundary between God's mercy and His wrath.

3. *Dew* sets forth the fertilizing, refreshing presence of the Holy Spirit. It comes from above. It is beneficial, saturating, silent in its operations.

4. *The Seal* indicates *security* of that or those sealed by the Spirit. It proclaims the fact of *ownership* and preciousness.
The Seal implies a finished transaction.

5. *The Earnest* proclaims the fact that what I am and have now is proof positive of what I shall

further have and be when I shall be like HIM whom having not seen I nevertheless love.

6. *Fire* is an emblem of purification. It sets forth the sanctifying energy of the Holy Spirit.
Fire purifies, unites, consumes, inflames, warms, cheers, fuses, assimilates, tests and illuminates. Fire is the sign of God in both the Old and New Testaments. The Burning Bush — The Mountain—The Pillar of Fire—Isaiah's fiery baptism—The Promised Baptism with the Holy Ghost and Fire—Matthew 3:11—Mark 1:8— Luke 3:16—John 1:33.

7. *Oil* speaks of the Holy Spirit as enlightening, lubricating, filling. Oil poured into wounds, filling the lampstand, flowing through the branches, causing faces to shine. Mingling with oil speaks of the Birth of the Spirit. Oil poured foreshadows Pentecost. Anointing with Oil prepares for service and success.

8. The Dove speaks of the beauty, gentleness, guilelessness of the Holy Spirit. The Dove is clean in nature, gentle in manner, constant in love, particular in food, swift, beautiful and social in habits.

> *O Holy Dove, thy life Divine*
> *To me in grace impart*
> *O make me live to God alone,*
> *And sanctify my heart.*

These emblems thus set forth the work of the Holy Spirit as

1. Mysterious
2. Invisible

3. Powerful
4. Cleansing
5. Purifying
6. Refreshing
7. Invigorating
8. Illuminating
9. Saturating
10. Uniting
11. Cheering
12. Lubricating

"Man was placed in the world like a king in a palace stored with all to please him, monarch and sovereign of all the lower orders of creation. The sun to labor for him like a very Hercules; the moon to light his nights, or lead the waters around the earth in tides, cleansing its shores; elements of nature to be his slaves and messengers; flowers to scent his pathway; fruit to please his taste; birds to sing for him; beasts to toil for him and carry him; and man himself, amid all this luxury, God's representative, his vice-gerent. This is man as God made him. We see him now as sin has made him. His crown is rolled in the dust and tarnished. His sovereignty is strongly disputed by the lower orders of creation. The earth supplies him with food only after arduous toil. The beasts serve him only after they have been laboriously tamed and trained, while vast numbers roam the forests, setting him at defiance. So degraded has man become through sin, that he has bowed before the objects that he was to command, and has prostrated his royal form at shrines dedicated to birds, and four-footed beasts, and creeping things."

F. B. Meyer.

4

REPLENISHMENT

*"And God said, Let us make man in our image, af-
ter our likeness; and let them have dominion over the
fish of the sea, and over the fowl of the air, and over
the cattle, and over all the earth, and over every creeping thing that creepeth upon the earth.*

*So God created man in his own image, in the image
of God created he him; male and female created he
them.*

*And God blessed them, and God said unto them,
Be fruitful, and multiply, and replenish the earth, and
subdue it; and have dominion over the fish of the sea,
and over the fowl of the air, and over every living
thing that moveth upon the earth"* Genesis 1: 26-28.

The earth was laid waste by sin and judgment, and
the Spirit of God brooded over the darkness. God
speaks and light came; the light was separated from the
darkness, for darkness and light cannot mix; the light
was called day and the darkness was called night, and
thus, the period known to us as *time* commenced. The
first day was born, for, "the evening and the morning
were the first day." In one of God's tomorrows TIME
shall be no more. The evening and the morning were the
FIRST day and some evening and some morning in the
future shall be the LAST day. The New Earth with
the New Heaven and the New City shall usher in an
eternal day without a night.

We draw your attention to the expression "The
evening and the morning were the first day." The

31

first day thus began with an evening and ended with a morning. God thus is able to begin in the darkness and to end in the light. Man begins in the light and ends in the dark.

The next step in the restoration of the ruined earth was the placing of an expanse or firmament called Heaven after which the earth or dry land appeared. The dry land was called *earth* and the waters were called *seas*. The tender grass began to grow, the fruit trees yielded fruit, the sun shone by day and the moon by night, and moving, living creatures soon filled the earth, the sea and the air. Then came the climax of all God's creative and restorative plans. The Trinity met together in sacred council and decided to climax creation with MAN, made in their own image and after their own likeness, and to give them dominion over the restored earth. No sooner was it decided than it was done; man was created in the image and likeness of God. A garden was planted in Eden, and amid scenes of exquisite beauty and delight and with everything to satisfy his God-like nature, man was placed in the garden and ordered by his Creator to dress and keep the garden. The command was thus given: "Be fruitful and multiply and REPLENISH the earth and subdue it and have dominion." Here is the doctrine of replenishification. The word replenish means to fill again. This command was given BEFORE the fall. The all too prevalent idea that babies are born into this world because of sin has absolutely no foundation in the scriptures. The original command to be fruitful and multiply and replenish the earth was given BEFORE the temptation and BEFORE the fall. It was always God's gracious will to fill the earth with holy, clean, pure and innocent children who would grow up to be holy, clean, pure and innocent men and women. This shall yet be accomplished.

God's purposes and plans having been completed, God rested from all His work which He created and made. This restoration of the ruined earth is an exact pen-picture of the ways of God in redemption. The Holy Spirit moves over the darkness of the soul, the Word of God is preached and LIGHT comes to the soul of man; then comes separation, resurrection, fruit-bearing and, at last, we stand before God in His own image and likeness.

The order is thus:

    (1) *Holiness* ....Genesis 1:1
    (2) Sin ....   "   1:2 (1st Clause)
    (3) The Holy Spirit ... "   1:2 (2nd Clause)
    (4) The Word Preached . "   1:3
    (5) Light .... "   1:4
    (6) Separation .... "   1:4-8
    (7) Resurrection .... "   1:9-10
    (8) Fruit .... "   1:11-13
    (9) Shining Lights ..... "   1:14-19
 (10) *Holiness* .... "   1:20-31

This is the way of God both in Nature and in Grace—holiness at the beginning and holiness at the end.

"Genesis has a character of its own; and, as the beginning of the Holy Book, presents to us all the great elementary principles which find their development in the history of the relationship of God with man, which is recorded in the following books. The germ of each of these principles will be found here, unless we except the law. There was however a law given to Adam in his innocence; and Hagar, we know, prefigures at least Sinai. There is scarce anything afterwards accomplished of which the expression is not found in this book in one form or another. There is found also in it, though the sad history of man's fall be there, a freshness in the relationship of man with God, which is scarce met with afterwards in men accustomed to abuse it and to live in a society full of itself. But whether it be the creation, man and his fall, sin, the power of Satan, the promises, the call of God, His judgment of the world, redemption, the covenants, the separation of the people of God, their condition of strangers on the earth, the resurrection, the establishment of Israel in the land of Canaan, the blessing of the nations, the seed of promise, the exaltation of a rejected Lord to the throne of the world, all are found here in fact or in figure—in figure, now that we have the key, even the church itself."

J. N. Darby
(Synopsis of the Books
of the Bible, p. 8)

5

THE FIRST BRIDE

"And the Lord God said, It is not good that the man should be alone; I will make him an help meet for him.

And out of the ground the Lord God formed every beast of the field, and every fowl of the air; and brought them unto Adam to see what he would call them: and whatsoever Adam called every living creature, that was the name thereof. And Adam gave names to all cattle, and to the fowl of the air, and to every beast of the field: but for Adam there was not found an help meet for him.

And the Lord God caused a deep sleep to fall upon Adam, and he slept: and he took one of his ribs, and closed up the flesh instead thereof;

And the rib, which the Lord God had taken from man, made he a woman, because she was taken out of Man.

Therefore shall a man leave his father and mother, and shall cleave unto his wife: and they shall be one flesh. And they were both naked, the man and his wife, and were not ashamed." Genesis 2:18-25.

God's plans and purposes for this earth are its re-plenishification with a holy, sinless race. Such shall yet be accomplished. There shall be new nations on the new earth, and Paradise lost in the fall, shall be fully restored and God's original plan will be fulfilled. When the bell rings down the curtain on the affairs of men, and TIME shall be no more, all the mischief wrought by sin will have been rectified by Christ and redemption, and the original command disobeyed in Eden lost will be obeyed in Eden restored. Victory is on the side of God and Holiness. Between Paradise lost and Paradise restored God calls out a special peculiar people called the Church, and from His church there will be chosen, elected, and selected, a Bride, and, after the Church and the Bride is completed, there shall be a new heaven without a Devil, and a new earth without a sinner, and the replenishification of the new earth will be accomplished by the new nations.

Adam was created holy, wise, innocent, perfect and God-like. The *wisdom* of Adam is seen in the fact of his giving names to all cattle and to the fowls of the air and to every beast of the field. They all loved and obeyed Adam and were all domesticates by creation. The lion was just as harmless as the lamb and the dinosaur as docile as the dove. The *holiness* of Adam is seen in the fact that he was created in the image and the likeness of God. The *innocence* of Adam is seen in the fact that he was not ashamed. Adam was put into a deep sleep, his side was opened, and from his wounded side there came forth his bride who was a type of the bride of Christ. Eve was in Adam before she became his bride; she was taken from his wounded side; she was taken from the place nearest his own loving heart; and she reigned and ruled with him over the restored creation. Eve, however, was only a very small part of Adam's body and this also has a spiritual meaning for us. The body of Christ is the Church and the Bride of Christ will be that part of His body which is nearest and dearest to His own loving heart. The Bride of Christ will reign and rule with Him over a restored creation just as Adam and Eve ruled together over a restored creation. The deep sleep of Adam was a fore-shadowing of the deep sleep of Christ on Calvary when His side was opened and from His wounded side there has flowed a crimson stream that even now is building His Bride. Jesus left His Father when He came down to earth to suffer and die; He left His Mother when he was on the cross, tenderly leaving her in charge of the beloved John. He left His Father and left His Mother and shall yet cleave to His Bride who even now is making herself ready and watching for the coming of the heavenly Bridegroom.

We would draw your attention here to a very beautiful truth. When the side of Adam was opened he was already in a deep sleep. Adam was unconscious when the wound was made in his side. Christ was already dead when His side was opened. When the wound was made in the side of Christ he was already dead and the soldier seeing he was dead pierced His side with the spear. Both Adam and Christ were unconscious when their sides were opened. There are eight Brides in the Bible and all are clearly typical of the Bride of Christ.

First Things

I. The first Work . . . CREATION . . . Genesis 1:1

>True account
>Not a single disclosure of Science against it
>Verified by New Testament
>No other satisfactory explanation

II. The first Sabbath

>Made for man
>Needful for Worship
>Essential for body and brain

III. The first Garden
>   Eden—delight
>   Lost in the fall
>   Destroyed by the flood
>   Restored by Christ

IV. The first Man
>   Dust and Deity

V. The first Stewardship
>   Man to dress and keep the garden

VI. The first Command
>   Only one command and hence simple and easy
>   A command to remind man of
>   1. his subordinate relation
>   2. his duty
>   3. his freedom

VII. The first Temptation
>   Temptation is not sin
>   Adam and Christ were holy
>   Moral beings must be tested

The Serpent . . . Genesis 3
>   "The old Serpent called the Devil and Satan." As Dan was a Serpent, Herod was a fox, and Judah was a lion's whelp; so Satan is likened to a serpent.
>   Never talk about the snake and apple business when dealing with the Ruin of the Race.
>   The word *apple* never once occurs in connection with the temptation and fall.
>   The word of God says *a serpent* NOT a snake.

Fruit NOT an apple.

The so-called Snake and Apple Business:

1. Hides God's Truth
2. Causes infidels to Sneer
3. Encourages the Critics
4. Stumbles the weak
5. Minimizes sin
6. Delights Satan
7. Condemns God.

VIII. The First Sin
Rebellion
Guilt
Lawlessness
Disobedience

IX. The First Curse
Upon the Serpent
Upon Eve
Upon Adam
Upon the ground

X. The first Gospel
Coat of Skins
Promise . . . Genesis 3:15

THE FALL

Genesis 3

Sin, like the cloud seen by Elijah, was small at first but finally spread until it covered the heavens.

Observe (1) The *Teachings of Satan*
"Ye shall not . . . die."

(2) Human reasoning
"She saw . . . coveted . . . took . . . gave."

    (3) Man made religion
        ". . . made themselves aprons."
    (4) Conscience at work
        "They hid themselves."
    (5) The Seeking Christ
        "Where art thou?"
    (6) Excuses
        "The woman thou gavest."
    (7) God ordained religion
        "God made . . . coats of skins . . ."
        Sacrifice
        Atonement
        Substitution
        Covering
        Salvation by Faith through Blood

Seven Results of the Fall

1. The ground was cursed.
    Christ was made a curse.
2. Sorrow became the lot of humans.
    Christ was the man of sorrows.
3. Sweat
    Christ sweat . . . blood.
4. Thorns and thistles
    Christ was given a crown of thorns.
5. Suffering and death
    Christ suffered and died.
6. The Sword to keep the way of the tree of life.
    Christ's side was pierced by the sword or spear and thus the way was opened to the tree of life.
7. Separation from God
    "My God . . . why . . . forsaken me?"

Man

I. The object of his life.

  Eph. 6:6—"Doing the will of God from the heart."

  John 6:38—"Not to do my own will, but the will of him that sent me."

  Heb. 10:7—"Lo I come to do thy will O God."

II. The study of his life.

  2 Tim. 2:15—"Study to shew thyself approved unto God."

  Eph. 5:17-18—"Understanding what the will of the Lord is . . . . be filled with the Spirit."

III. The ambition of his life.

  Phil. 4:18—"Well pleasing to God."

IV. The sustenance of his life.

  John 4:34—"My meat is to do the will of him that sent me."

V. The Joy of his life.

  Psa. 40:8—"I delight to do thy will."

  Psa. 1—"His delight is in the law of the Lord."

VI. The Prayer of his life.

  Matt. 6:10—"Thy will be done in earth."

VII. The End of his life.

  Psa. 37:37—"Mark the perfect man (perfect love) and behold the upright (life) for the end of that man is peace."

"Man Became a Living Soul"

Genesis 2:7

1. The Soul
   a. Understanding
   b. Judgment

      c.   Imagination
      d.   Conscience
      e.   Will
      f.   Emotions

2:   The Endlessness of the Soul
      a.   A Spiritual entity
      b.   The universal desire and longing of man
      c.   There is *no annihilation* either in nature or grace.

3.   Illustrated and Exemplified
      a.   Enoch
      b.   Elijah
      c.   Moses
      d.   Rich man and Lazarus
      e.   Samuel and Saul

THE FIRST MARRIAGE

Genesis 2

1.   The Man
      a.   Adam
      b.   Christ
"It is not good that *the* man should be alone."

2.   The Woman
      a.   Eve
      b.   The Bride of Christ
          Bow-builded
          God's gift
          God's image

3.   The Sleep
      a.   Adam's deep sleep
      b.   Christ's death on the Cross
          Sleep is the figure of Death.

4. Resurrection
   a.   Adam
   b.   Christ
   Adam was put into a deep sleep.
   His side was opened.
   His bride was builded.
   He was unconscious when his side was opened.
   It was the same with Christ.
   (1)   His deep sleep of death.
   (2)   His side opened.
   (3)   He was dead when his side was opened.
   (4)   He was awakened out of his deep sleep or death (Resurrection).
   (5)   His Bride is being builded (NOT EVOLVED).

5. The Marriage
   a.   "Jehovah brought her unto *the man.*"
   b.   "One with him 'Bone of my bone'."
   c.   "Christ left his Father in Heaven and left his mother with John on earth to cleave to his bride and wife.

"WHERE ART THOU?"

Genesis 3:9

Ten Great Bible Questions:
   1.   Where are thou? .... to Adam
   2.   Where is thy Brother? .... to Cain
   3.   What hast thou done? .... to Cain
   4.   Can these bones live? .... to Ezekiel
   5.   Wilt thou go with this man? ...... to Rebekah
   6.   What think ye of Christ? .... to disciples
   7.   What shall I do then with Jesus? ....
        .... Pilate's question

8. What shall it profit? .... Mark 8:36
9. How shall we escape? .... Heb. 2:3
10. Where is the Lord God of Elijah?..II Kings 2:14

THE FIRST JUDGMENT SCENE

I. The flight of the Criminals
    1. Instinct of Sinful to run away from God
        a. Because of guilt
        b. Dread of punishment
    2. The habit of God to seek for the sinner
        Adam
        Jonah
        David
        Prodigal
    3. All fugitives eventually arrested
        Adam and Eve
        Cain
        David
        Ahab
        Jonah

II. The examination of the Criminals
    1. God's searching questions?
        Where art thou?
        Who told thee?
    2. Man's weak excuses
        Adam blamed Eve
        Eve blamed the Serpent
    3. The Divine Verdict

III. The Sentence of the Criminals
    1. On the Serpent
    2. On the Woman
    3. On the man

The First Brothers

Genesis 4: 1-16

1. The brothers at home
2. The brothers at work
      (1)   Necessary
      (2)   Various
      (3)   Useful
      (4)   Healthful
3. The brothers at worship
4. The brothers at war
      (1)   Unseemly
      (2)   Unjustifiable
      (3)   Murderous
5. The brothers at the judgment bar

The Way of Cain

1. The Way of human reason
   The best he knew . . . he had
2. The Way of unconfessed sin
   First fruits of a cursed ground
   No confession and no Blood
3. The Way of insanity
   "Cain was very wroth . . ."
4. The Way of Childishness
   "His countenance fell . . ."
5. The Way of Murder
6. The Way of Condemnation
   "Now art thou cursed."
7. The Way of Despair
   "Mine iniquity is greater than it may be forgiven."
8. The Way of Banishment from God
   "He went out . . . ."

THE WAY OF CAIN

I. His own Way
1. Of hatred
2. Self Righteousness
3. Defiance
II. His Privileges
1. Believing Parents
2. A Wise and pious Brother
3. A gracious God
III. His Doom
1. His Sin
2. His despair
3. His departure

"The Book of Genesis is in many respects the most important book in the Bible. It is of the first importance because it answers, not exhaustively, but sufficiently, the fundamental questions of the human mind. It contains the first authoritative information given to the race concerning these questions of everlasting interest: the Being of God; the origin of the universe; the creation of man; the origin of the soul; the fact of revelation; the introduction of sin; the promise of salvation; the primitive division of the human race; the purpose of the elected people; the preliminary part in the program of Christianity. In one word, in this inspired volume of beginnings, we have the satisfactory explanation of all the sin and misery and contradiction now in this world, and the reason of the scheme of redemption."

6

TEN NAMES AND THEIR MEANINGS

All names in the Bible have a spiritual and practical meaning for us today. All changes of names in the Bible have also lessons for us in this dispensation. The ten names of Genesis five set forth at least seven thousand years of sacred history.

The first name is Adam.

ADAM means "red earth." Adam was neither a white man nor a black (colored) man nor a yellow or brown man. Adam or red earth speaks to us of the natural man, man by nature away from God and righteousness and holiness.

The second name is Seth.

SETH means "Substitute." Cain murdered his brother Abel and Seth was given instead of Abel and thus Seth speaks of Christ as the Substitute for fallen man. Christ is our Substitute.

The third name is Enos.

ENOS means "frailty, mortality or dying" and speaks of Christ dying for us. Seth speaks of the Substitute and Enos speaks of the Substitute dying; the just for the unjust, and the innocent for the guilty. The Ram caught in the thicket by its horns was a substitute for Isaac and the ram was taken and offered instead of Isaac, the ram died that Isaac might live and Christ our Substitute (Seth) died (Enos) that we might have life and have it more abundantly.

The fourth name is Cainan.

CAINAN means "to purchase, to buy back, to acquire." When Christ died He purchased us out of the slave market of sin and through His atoning blood bought back all and more than Adam lost in the garden of Eden. Christ not only became our Substitute dying for us, but in His death and through His death He purchased the field which is the world and also the treasure in the field and thus He became our Cainan, buying back that which Adam lost in the fall.

The fifth name is Mahalaleel.

MAHALALEEL means "the splendor of God." Christ our Substitute (Seth) died for us (Enos) and bought back that which Adam lost (Cainan) was resurrected from the dead, "the splendor of God" in resurrection power and thus He became our Mahalaleel.

The sixth name is Jared.

JARED means "to pour out, to descend." Christ, after His resurrection, ascended on high, received the promise of the Father and poured out the gift of the Holy Ghost upon the waiting apostles on the day of Pentecost. Thus Christ became our Jared. This brings us to the present age or dispensation which is the dispensation of the Spirit. Before Jesus died He promised the Comforter to his people and said that when the Comforter was come He would teach them all things and instruct them in the things of God.

The seventh name is Enoch.

ENOCH means "to teach or to instruct." We are now living in the Enoch age or dispensation. The Holy Ghost has come to instruct, to teach and to lead us into all the truth. Enoch was translated that he might not see death, and before his translation he walked with

God, enjoyed the witness that he was righteous, and was raptured without passing through the valley of the shadow of death.

The number seven in the Bible is the number of perfection and Enoch is the seventh name mentioned in the chapter. He was translated that he might not see death.

The number six in the Bible is the number of evil, and Jared is the sixth name mentioned in the chapter. Jared (Pentecost) ushered in the present dispensation which abounds in evil. This present dispensation will end with the rapture of the saints just as Enoch was raptured. It is now our privilege and joy to walk with God and like Enoch live a holy life although in the midst of sin.

Enoch was a foreshadow type of all those who will be alive and remain unto the coming of the Lord.

1. The times in which he lived were full of evil.

2. He walked with God.
    (1) Harmony
    (2) Unity
    (3) Fellowship

3. He enjoyed the Witness of the Holy Spirit.
    "He had this testimony that he pleased God."
    Heb. 11:5.

4. He was a living rebuke to sin.
    "He testified of judgment." Jude 14.

5. He was a preacher of righteousness.
    "Enoch prophesied saying."

6. He was translated.
    "God took him."

The next name is Methuselah.

METHUSELAH means "when he is dead it shall be sent." Enoch walked with God. God revealed to him a secret. God told Enoch that He was about to judge the world for its iniquity, He was about to sweep the earth with the besom of destruction because of its awful sin. God revealed to Enoch that a flood was to be sent upon the earth, and Enoch believed God although he had never seen either snow or rain or a flood. A son was born to Enoch and the name given to the boy was Methuselah, which means, *when he is dead it shall be sent.* Methuselah lived to the ripe old age of 969 years and when he died the flood was sent upon the earth. Infidels mock and jeer because of the great age of Methuselah, while the devout student and Christian rejoices and praises God. God lengthened out the brittle thread of that one man's life almost a millennium because at his death the race was to be swept from the earth with a flood. Thus is revealed to the devout student the marvelous long-suffering of God who is not willing that any should perish. Judgment being His strange work, He seemingly hesitated to strike the blow which would destroy the race and thus Methuselah lived on and on and on until at last even Methuselah died and God's Judgments burst upon the earth. After the Enochs of this present dispensation are resurrected and raptured the great tribulation will burst upon the earth. The flood in the Old Testament was a fore-shadowing of the great tribulation.

The next name is Lamech.

LAMECH means "conqueror or king." After the rapture of the saints and the great tribulation Christ is coming to the earth as its conquering King and the millennial day of rest and peace shall begin. This brings us to the last name on the list which is Noah.

NOAH means "rest." Christ our substitute (Seth) died for us (Enos) and bought back all and more than was lost in the fall (Cainan). He rose again (Mahalaleel), ascended on high and poured out the Holy Ghost (Jared) Who has come to cleanse and fill and also instruct us in the things of God during this dispensation (Enoch). This dispensation will end with the rapture and then will begin the period called the great tribulation, ending with the coming of the Conquering King of Kings and Lord of Lords (Lamech) and the commencement of the millennial reign of Christ upon the earth (Noah). Here are set forth in ten names over seven thousand years of sacred history, and each name contains at least one good message or sermon:

1. Man by nature .... Adam
2. Substitution .... Seth
3. The death of Christ .... Enos
4. Redemption or Atonement .... Cainan
5. The resurrection of Christ .... Mahalaleel
6. Pentecost .... Jared
7. The present age .... Enoch
8. The great tribulation .... Methuselah
9. The coming King .... Lamech
10. The Millennium .... Noah

"There is a sweet simplicity in the narratives of this first book that is very attractive to little children, and there is a depth in them that lies beyond the reach of the profoundest minds. It forms the preface of the entire Bible, for it contains the germ of all subsequent revelations, until we reach the Apocalypse, which is the equally striking conclusion of the inspired Scriptures. Hence there is a remarkable correspondence between the two books; the paradise of God, the tree of life, the river, the crown of sovereignty upon man's brow seen in the former, reappearing in the latter; and the blessings lost in the first Adam restored in the last Adam in the very order in which they disappeared. Thus the Holy Ghost at once exhibits the perfect unity of His word, and teaches us not only to "search the scriptures," but to search them until Christ is revealed to the heart in all the glory of his divine person, and in all the value of His finished work."

James H. Brookes
(An outline of the books of the Bible, p. 7)

7

NOAH, THE ARK AND THE DELUGE

"But Noah found grace in the eyes of the Lord."
Genesis 6:8.

The wickedness of man waxed great in the earth
and in order to give the race a new lease of life God
ordered Noah to prepare an ark to the salvation of himself and his household. The ark was made of wood
with three stories, a window in the top and a door in
the side. It was pitched inside and outside with pitch.
God himself entered into the ark and called Noah to
enter therein. The fountains of the deep were broken
up. The heavens were opened and the ship was borne
on the rising waters. The waves lashed the ship on
every side. The waters prevailed until the wicked race
was swept from the face of the earth. All inside the
ship were saved and all outside of the ship perished.
All inside the ark were taken up and all who were
taken up came back to the earth again.

The ark was typical of our Lord Jesus Christ. The
wood sets forth the humanity of Christ, wood being obtained from a tree which has been cut down, sawed,
hammered and nailed to provide an ark to save the
race alive. The living tree, having received a certain
amount of nourishment from the ground or from
mother nature, must surrender its life before an ark
can be built. Thus the wood of the ark fore-shadows
our Lord Jesus Christ, as the living tree of righteousness cut down to provide a place of safety for the human race. The ark was pitched inside and outside with
pitch and this sets forth the shed blood of our Lord

Jesus Christ. Had it not been for the pitch the judgment waters would have entered the ark and Noah and his sacred freight would have all gone down in the deluge. The wood alone which sets forth our Lord's humanity could not have kept out the judgment waters. There must be not only the wood but also the pitch, the shed blood of Christ. The window which was around the top of the ark teaches us to look up and unto Jesus the "author and finisher of our faith." The door or opening in the side of the ark foreshadows the wounded side of Christ. Noah entered into the ark through the opening in its side, in fact, all who were saved in the flood entered and were saved because of the opening in the side of the ark. Just so, all who are saved today must enter in through the open side, even the side that was pierced on Calvary's rugged tree. Adam's side was opened in order to obtain a bride, the side of the ark was opened in order to save the race and it is through the opening in the side of our Ark, Jesus Christ, that a sinful race may be saved.

The three stories in the ark set forth the tripartite nature of our Lord Jesus Christ—spirit, soul and body.

Then the waters from beneath were first broken up. It is interesting to notice that the Bible says the waters from beneath were broken up first and then the heavens were opened. This sets forth the fact that all Hell was enraged against Christ the Ark. The waters from beneath foreshadow the vengeance and venom of Hell that spent itself on the spotless Son of God. The windows of heaven were then opened and this sets forth the sufferings of Christ having been made a curse for us. He, our Ark, bore the wrath of an offended Deity. The windows of heaven were opened upon Him for "it pleased the Lord to bruise him, he hath put him to grief—." The lashings by the waves on every side of the ark foreshadow the sufferings of Christ as endured by Him from the scourging, beatings and smitings of man. The waters from beneath foreshadow the vengeance of hell, the waters from above foreshadow the wrath of God to be poured out upon the sacred head of the Ark, and the waves around as they lash the ark foreshadow the smitings of man who hit Him with their fists, smote Him with the reed and otherwise mocked and jeered the immaculate Son of God and Son of Man.

The wood, the pitch, the hammerings, the nails and the door all set forth the sufferings of Christ to provide a place for safety for sinful man. Just as all inside the ark were saved and all outside the ark perished, so it is today. By repentance and faith we enter into our ark, Christ Jesus, and only in Christ is there safety. All outside the ark perished so all outside of Christ must perish. Again, just as all inside the ark were taken up, so we shall be caught up "to meet the Lord in the air and so shall we ever be with Him." Again, all who were taken up came back to earth again. This foreshadows the coming to the earth of Christ with His saints to reign and rule in millennial power and glory. The Ark rested on Ararat.

The first chapter of Genesis ends with rest. The fifth chapter of Genesis ends with rest. The story of the flood ends with rest. Noah went forth from the ark to rule and reign over a purified creation. Those who are in Christ will be caught up. Those who are caught up will come back to the earth again and with Christ shall reign over a purified creation.

We call the attention of the reader to the fact that there were more besides Noah in the ark. Shem, Ham and Japheth were in the ark. The hog was in the ark as well as the lamb. The raven was in the ark as well as the dove. All this has a meaning for us. Shem, the representative of the Jewish race, was saved in the ark. Ham, the representative of the colored race, was in the ark. Japheth, the representative of the white race, was saved in the ark. The hog was saved as well as the lamb and the raven and the dove. This foreshadows the fact that in a day that is yet to come all Israel shall be saved and the colored race shall be saved and the white race shall be saved and the grunt shall be taken from the hog and the ferocity from the tiger and the lion. The lion shall then lie down with the lamb and "They shall not hurt nor destroy in all my holy mountain." There have been many dispensations past such as the dispensations of conscience, law and promise. There is the present dispensation of grace. There will be a future dispensation of judgment and righteousness and all these are foreshadowed in the story of Noah, the ark and the flood. Noah represents the holy people who are saved in this age or dispensation. Noah was righteous, holy, perfect, just and good. The close of this dispensation will not be the end of the world. There are other dispensations yet to come. In the future all Israel will be saved. From the rising of the sun to the going down of the same, Righteousness shall cover the earth and redemption shall be enjoyed by the beasts of the field, the fish of the seas and the fowls of the air. The groan shall be taken out of creation and Paradise lost in the fall shall be restored through the redemption that is in Jesus. In this age men must repent, confess their sins, accept Christ as their Saviour, make all necessary restitution, and walk in the light, obtain the Baptism with the

Holy Ghost and fire, live in obedience to God and like Noah be saved by virtue of our Lord Jesus Christ, our Ark. As Paul was converted by a personal revelation of Jesus Christ to him, so the Jews will be saved by a personal revelation to Christ to them. Then Christ will set up His millennial kingdom and all men everywhere for a thousand years shall enjoy the benefits of Christ's atoning blood.

THE DAYS OF NOAH

1. Distinguished for inventions, arts and science.
   Tubal Cain and his weapons
   Jubal with his music, etc.
2. Unbelief
   "They knew not until the flood came."
   Noah's preaching and acting
   Man's unbelief and sin
3. Wickedness
   The cup of iniquity was full.
4. Violence
   "The earth was filled with violence."
5. Sensualism and divorce
   "They took them wives of all which they chose."
6. Intemperance
   ". . . eating and drinking . . ."
7. Worldliness
   ". . . they bought . . . sold . . . planted . . . builded . . ."
8. The people were forewarned of their danger.
9. Only a few prepared for the deluge.
10. There came a moment when it was too late.
    "The door was shut."

"As . . . IN THE DAYS OF NOAH"

Genesis 6:1-8

1. Licentiousness raging
   1. Marriage between Sethites and Cainites
   2. Married to please their fancies
   3. Married as often as they desired
2. Violence prevailing
3. Corruption deepening
4. Grace operating
   "Noah found grace."
5. Judgment descending
   "Come thou and all thy house into the Ark."
   1. A timely invitation .... Come
   2. A special invitation .... Thou
   3. A comprehensive invitation .... All
   4. A gracious invitation .... The Lord said
   5. An urgent invitation .... Seven (7) days

THE DELUGE

1. The Divine sentence or decisions
   "The end of all flesh . . . I will destroy."
2. The Divine Design
   "Make an Ark."
3. The Divine Warning
   "Behold I . . . . will bring a flood."
4. The Divine Invitation
   "Come . . ."
5. The Divine Security
   "The Lord shut him in."
6. The Divine Remembrance
   "The Lord remembered Noah."

7.   The Divine Commission
        "Go forth"
        "In" for salvation
        "Forth" for Testimony
        "Come in . . . and . . . Go forth."

God's Ark

Genesis 7:1-7

1.   God's way of salvation
2.   God's only way of salvation
3.   A place of Security—"The Lord shut him in."
4.   A place of Separation
5.   A place of Sufficiency
6.   Accepted by Some
        1.   Noah
        2.   Noah's wife
        3.   Noah's sons
        4.   Noah's sons' wives
     "Come thou and all thy house."
     "Believe . . . and thou . . . and thy house."
     "The promise is unto you . . . Children."
7.   Rejected by others
        1.   Talking about the Ark cannot save
        2.   Looking at it cannot save
        3.   Desire to enter cannot save

THE JUDGMENT OF GOD

Genesis 8:1-14

I.   God's judgment have their specified purposes.
        1.   Separation of righteous from wicked.
        2.   Tares and Wheat
        3.   Good and bad fish

II. God's judgments have their appointed times.
    1. The time of the flood
    2. The destruction of Jerusalem
    3. The end of the world

III. God's judgments have their appropriate signs.
    1. The growing wickedness of men
    2. The preparations of the righteous
    3. The restlessness of the nations

"As It Was in the Days of Noah"

1. Multiplication of Mankind.
2. God was longsuffering toward them.
3. God sent Messengers to warn . . . . (Enoch) (Noah).
4. God's Spirit strove with them.
5. God warned that His Spirit would not always strive.
6. God's word was despised and rejected.
7. A few found Grace . . . (Enoch) (Noah).
8. Enoch was miraculously translated.
9. Fallen angels united with the race—SPIRITISM.
10. God's wrath was poured out.

"The Book of Genesis is the most ardent history in the world; and, from the great variety of its singular details and most interesting accounts, is as far superior in its value and importance to others, as it is in its antiquity.

"The book contains an account of the creation of the world, and its first inhabitants; the original innocence and fall of man; the rise of religion; the invention of arts; the general corruption and degeneracy of mankind; the universal deluge; the repeopling and division of the earth; the origin of nations and kingdoms; and a particular history of the *patriarchs* from *Adam* down to the death of *Joseph,* including a space, at the lowest computation, of two thousand, three hundred sixty-nine (2369) years."

ADAM CLARKE
(Preface to the Book
of Genesis)

8

NIMROD

"Let us build us . . . and let us make us a name."
Genesis 11:4.

After the flood Noah took of every clean beast and of every clean fowl and offered burnt offerings unto the Lord. The Lord accepted the worship and sacrifice, and in His heart decided never again to curse the ground for man's sake and that while the earth remaimed, seed time and harvest, and cold and heat, and summer and winter, and day and night should not cease. Then he commanded the race to scatter abroad upon the face of the earth. The whole earth was of one language and one speech. Instead of scattering abroad they found a plain in the land of Shinar and they dwelt there. They then decided and determined to make brick, build a tower and a city, and make themselves a name. In two verses they used the word *us* five times and never once mentioned the name of God. The Lord came down to see the city and the tower, for God is interested in the doings of man. To restrain them from further sin and wickedness God confounds their language so that they could not understand one another's speech, and thus they were scattered abroad upon the face of the earth. This first attempt to establish a godless civilization was thwarted by the direct interposition of God.

In Genesis eleven we have the first attempt of man to set up and establish a godless society. Cain was the first person to name a city after the name of his own son. Lamech was the first polygamist and the second murderer. Ham was the first backbiter and slanderer, and Nimrod was the first man to start a godless civilization. Babel or Babylon was the result at the beginning as it will be the result in the end. The first Babylon is seen in Genesis and the last Babylon is seen in Revelation.

The first egotist in all the universe was Lucifer; the first day began with a night; the first marriage ceremony was performed by God; the first liar was Satan; the first trifler with the Word of God was Eve; the first murderer was Cain; the first person to die was Abel; the first person to escape death was Enoch and the first society-man and city builder was Nimrod. God never made a brick, never built anything with bricks and never commanded anyone else to build anything with bricks. Without the Bible we are without any knowledge of the first two thousand years of the history of the world. Apart from the Bible the most important part of the history of the human family is absolutely unknown and apart from the Bible we are without knowledge of either the past or the future.

9

THE WAY OF FAITH AND SEPARATION

"Get thee out." Genesis 12:1.

The story of Abram, which begins with Genesis Twelve, sets forth the way of faith and separation. There is seen

I. A sevenfold separation

    1. From Country
    2.   "   Kindred (relatives)
    3.   "   Father's house (loved ones)
    4.   "   Lot (Nephew)
    5.   "   Ishmael (Son)
    6.   "   Isaac (beloved Son)
    7.   "   Sarah (Wife)

Abraham's life is the pattern life of faith. He was called upon to die out to his country, his relatives, his home, and live a separated life unto God. Godless, unsaved relatives will not help us to God or heaven. The only way to win is to live a life of separation.

God separated the light from the darkness in the beginning and in God's thoughts and plans the darkness has always been separated from the light. Light and darkness cannot mix. There is no fellowship between the darkness and the light. When God called Abraham out of Ur of the Chaldees he called him to a life of complete separation. Separation was commanded and then the promises were given. It was Abraham, the separated one, who rescued Lot, the mixer. It is the separated man today who alone has the power to help and save the lost. Lot was a good man in Sodom, but mixed up with the things of Sodom he lost his influence even over his own family and almost lost his soul. His wife was doomed, his daughters were disgraced, and he cursed the world with Moabites and Ammonites. He was a good mixer, and in the gamble of mixing, he lost.

The bride of Isaac was to be found at a well drawing sparkling, refreshing water, and not at the movies, etc.

Israelites in Egypt were in slavery and bondage. Exodus means GOING OUT (Separation). Moses refused to be called the son of Pharaoh's daughter. He left the palace, choosing rather to suffer affliction with the people of God, than to enjoy the pleasures of sin for a season, esteeming the reproach of Christ greater riches than the treasures in Egypt for he had respect unto the recompense of the reward. Rejecting all the compromises of Pharaoh and determining that not a hoof should be left behind, he forsook Egypt, not fearing the wrath of the king. He endured, as seeing Him who is invisible.

It has always been God's will for His people to be a separated people, and as long as Israel was separated they were victorious. They departed from God, and demanded a king, to be like the nations around them, and thus the very thing that God did not want them to become was the very thing that they demanded. God wanted them to be His special, peculiar, royal, holy, separated people, but they wanted to be like the people around them. God's call is always to a life of separation from the world with all its fashions, foibles, fol-de-rols, fiddle-de-dees and follies.

A ship is all right in the sea, but the sea is all

wrong in the ship. The church is all right in the world, but the world is all wrong in the church.

Pharaoh did his best to keep God's people in Egypt, and Satan will do his best to keep us in the world.

The Nazarites in the Old Testament were a separated people, abstaining from wine and every other exciting pleasure. They bore reproach as separated ones, and there is still a reproach to the cross of Christ and full salvation.

Plowing with an unclean ass and a clean ox was forbidden.

Sowing divers seeds in a field was positively prohibited.

The unregenerated seeds of evil doers are to be separated from God's regenerated seeds. *Unclean* asses and *clean* oxen are not to be yoked together. The error of Balaam was nothing more or less than mixing the seed of Israel with the seed of Moab in order to get Balak's gold. Balaam has gone down into eternal infamy, because, knowing the will of God, he refused to do it. Samson lost his power, and lost his liberty, and lost his eyes, because he rested his consecrated head on the unholy lap of Delilah. (Type of the World). When the separated locks of Samson were clipped by the worldly Delilah, the Holy Ghost was finally grieved, and Samson became the laughing stock of his enemies. This Satan deceived world has always clubbed its godly Abels, laughed and jeered and mocked its righteous Noahs, scoffed its holy Isaacs, and thrown its devoted Daniels into dens of lions. It has always persecuted its pious Shadrachs and chopped the head from the shoulders of its rebuking John the Baptists. It has always imprisoned its Pauls and crucified its saviors. The unrighteous Hamans will always seek the destruction of the righteous Mordecais. No man can serve two masters is as true today as it was true yesterday. The lovers of pleasure more than lovers of God are as numerous today as they were yesterday. If we live and walk and talk and act as the saints of whom the world was not worthy, the same world that persecuted them will oppose and persecute us. The weak, spineless, jelly-fish, soft, sentimental, sickly professionalism of this day and age will never stir either God or Satan, men or devils. If we keep clean enough and straight enough and spiritual enough, we shall never be popular enough to be even desired by a Christ rejecting, sin loving, pleasure seeking world. "Thou shalt not sow thy field with mingled seed; neither shall a garment of linen and woolen come upon thee." Lev. 19:19.

"Be not conformed to this world."

"Come out from among them and be ye separate."

"From such turn away."

"They are not of the world even as I am not of the world."

II. Two Crises
      1. 75 years of Age
      2. 99 years of Age

Abraham had two crises or epochs in his experience. He was justified freely at the age of seventy-five and sanctified wholly when he was ninety-nine years old.

III. Five Mistakes
      1. Terah
      2. Lot
      3. Egypt
      4. Hagar
      5. Gerar

Abraham made five great mistakes. When God commanded him to GET OUT it was to be away from Terah and Lot, but he took his father and allowed Lot to follow. Lot caused him much pain and they finally separated. Lot wanted tall grass and fat cows. While he was looking at green grass, Abraham was looking at the scintillating stars; while Lot was busying himself with cows, Abraham was having communion with the Creator of the cows. This is the way of faith. Abraham was a star surveyor while Lot was a grass gazer. Lot considered gold while Abraham considered God. Abraham however stepped out of the path of faith by going down to Egypt. Circumstances in the way of a famine caused his departure for Egypt. He did not realize it is better to die of starvation in Canaan than to live in luxury in Egypt. The scare-crow of the poor farm is ever in the field which is the world. Better endure a few hardships in Canaan than be at ease in Egypt. We always take a step down when we go to Egypt for help or food.

The fourth mistake in the life of Abraham was in connection with Hagar. Eve listened to the serpent. Adam listened to Eve. Abraham listened to Sarah, took Hagar and Ishmael was born. Ishmael would never have been born if Abraham had listened to God. Selah!

There are thousands of people now dead who should have yet been alive, and there are thousands of people living who should never have been born.

God never made a devil, a mule, or a sinner.

The unspeakable Turk like the Moabites and Ammonites should never have been born.

Abraham's fifth mistake was in staying on the border of Gerar. Here is a warning against world-bordering. Abraham learned his lessons, however, profited by his mistakes and we are to follow the footsteps *of that faith* of our father Abraham. Avoid the steps of disobedience and unbelief and follow the steps of that faith without which it is impossible to please God.

Thus we have

    1. A sevenfold separation

    2. A twofold crisis

    3. Five great mistakes

IV. A sevenfold Promise.

    1. A great inheritance

    2. A great posterity

    3. A great name

    4. A great blessing

    5. A great alliance

    6. A great defiance

    7. A great influence

See Gen. 12:1-3.

ABRAHAM

The life of Faith

1. Faith halting

   Abram stops at Haran.

2. Faith tested

   The bread and butter question.

3. Faith triumphant

   He went back to the place from whence he went down.

   He also later rescued LOT.

4. The Generosity of Faith

   Abraham gave LOT his choice of the land.

5. Faith presumptuous

   Hagar and Ishmael.

6. Sanctifying Faith
   Abram to Abraham.
   "Walk before me . . . perfect." Gen. 17:1.
7. Faith interceding
   Plea for Sodom.
8. The lapse of Faith
   Abraham called Sarah his sister.
9. The supreme devotion of Faith
   The offering of Isaac.
10. The reward of Faith
   Isaac offered, resurrected in a figure, married to Rebekah, Jacob born, Israel becomes the chosen nation, and then from Israel, Christ is born.

ABRAHAM'S DESCENT INTO EGYPT

Genesis 12:10-20

I. The story of a good man's fall
   1. Disappointment
   2. Declining in faith
   3. Going into danger
   4. Resorting to worldly policy
   5. Practicing deception
   6. Looking after self

II. The story of a good man's Protection
   1. God protected Sarai
   2. God delivered both in His own time and way.

III. The story of a good man's reproof
   1. By his own conscience
   2. By a Sinner
   3. By God

"I AM THY SHIELD, AND THY EXCEEDING GREAT REWARD"
Genesis 15:1

I. God our shield

Man needs protection, for his life is a struggle.

1. Man needs protection against the forces of nature.
2. Man needs protection against disease on every hand.
3. Man needs protection against himself.
4. Man needs protection against the world.
5. Man needs protection against Satan.

II. God our reward

Life is not in vain. Sacrifice will not go unrewarded.

1. Moses looked forward to the reward
2. Christ
3. Paul

ABRAHAM
Genesis 17:1

1 A Divine Visitation
"The Lord appeared"
2. A Divine Revelation
"I am the Almighty God"
3. A Divine Declaration
"Walk before me"
4. A Divine Command
"Be thou perfect"

ABRAHAM—A TYPE OF CHRIST

1. Kinsman of those whom he delivered.
2. Undertook the emancipation of his brethren.
3. Despoiled the principalities and powers of evil.

4. Love was the impelling power.
5. His promptitude and celerity in hastening to the rescue.
6. Undertook a costly campaign.
7. Suffered in order to save.
8. Refused worldly gain.
9. Rejected the offer of the prince of Sodom.
10. Complete Victory.

ABRAHAM'S SERVANTS A TYPE OF THE CHURCH

I. A little army
   "Fear not little flock"
   "God's strength is made perfect in weakness"
II. Had many enemies
   1. Formidable
   2. Proud
   3. Boastful
III. They were united
   Trusty confederates
IV. Made a rapid forced march
   Earnest
   No time for delay
V. Acted skillfully
   Wise as serpents
VI. Triumphant
   1. Certain
   2. Complete
   3. Final

MELCHISEDEK—THE HIGH PRIEST

1. Appointed and called of God
2. Consecrated
   "For their sakes I sanctify (Consecrate, dedicate, set apart, sanctify) myself that they also

might be sanctified" (truly sanctified, made holy).

3. Holy
4. Faithful
5. Offered a Sacrifice to Jehovah
6. Made reconciliation for Sins
7. Brought God and Man together
8. Was able to sympathize with others
9. Interceded for transgressors
10. Blessed the people

Both Melchisedek and Aaron were thus types of our Lord Jesus Christ as our High Priest.

Melchisedek, the priest king, was a type of Christ as the Priestly-King. Moses was a prophet, Aaron was a priest, and David was a king. All three together fore-shadowed Christ as prophet, priest and King. Melchisedek, however, is the only individual priest king type in the Bible. He was king of righteousness and king of peace. He was without Father and without Mother and without beginning of days or end of life. He administered to Abraham the sacred emblems of the broken body and shed blood and thus Abraham received this New Testament sacrament in Old Testament times. Melchisedek not only administered the holy sacrament, but he received tithes from Abraham. In all this he was a type of Christ, for the tithe is the Lord's. Melchisedek was a fore-ordained shadow of the great substance, our present Priest, interceding for us on high, and our coming King.

To get the most out of Genesis, as well as a number of the other books of the Old Testament, much attention should thus be given to the study of *TYPES*. *One veiled figure in the congregation* will solicit more attention and excite more questions than any other per-

son present, be they ever so handsome or beautiful.
God has endowed us with a nature that seeks to lift
the veil. In many of the characters of the Old Testament Christ is veiled.

A type is like the shadow of an object reflected on
the wall. The shape and size of the shadow varies according to the angle the light falls on the object, and
according to the distance the object is from the source
of the light.

LESSONS FROM THE LIFE OF LOT

I. What He did
   1. He looked
        "Lot lifted up his eyes"—Gen. 13:10.
   2. He chose
        "Chose . . . . all the plain"—Gen. 13:11.
   3. He journeyed
        "Lot journeyed east"—Gen. 13:11.
   4. He pitched
        "His tent towards Sodom"—Gen. 13:12.
   5. He lingered
        "While he lingered"—Gen. 19:16.

II. What He Lost
   1. His testimony
        "Seemed as one that mocked"—Gen.
        19:14.
   2. His wife
        "A pillar of salt"—Gen. 19:26.
   3. His communion
        No communion in Sodom.
   4. His property
        Went in rich, came out poor.
   5. Nearly lost his life
        Was urged to leave—Gen. 19:22.

"The angels hastened Lot"
Genesis 19:15-16

These angels teach us how to deal with men.

1. We must go to their homes
   "They turned in unto Lot."
2. Proclaim the Truth
   "The Lord will destroy the place."
3. Exhort, urge and persuade
   "Up, get out of this place."
4. Pull them out of the Fire
   "The men laid hold upon his hand."
5. Arouse to a sense of immediate danger and need of action.
   "The angels hastened Lot."
   "Escape for thy life."

The Angels Hastened Lot
Genesis 19:15

I. Sinners need to be hastened
   1. Settled down
   2. Apt to linger
   3. Bound by many ties
      a. Family ties
      b. Business ties
   4. Delay means destruction
II. Saints need to be hastened
   1. Their need of holiness
      a. Essential for purity and power
      b. Necessary for heaven
   2. In matters of obedience
   3. In seeking the welfare of others . . . v. 12
III. Why they need to be hastened
   1. The flesh is weak
   2. The enemy is deadening

Abraham and Lot

Points of Contrast

Abraham a pilgrim sitting at the tent door. Lot a dweller in Sodom.

Abraham had three visitors, one of whom was the Lord. Lot had only two.

Abraham ran. Lot sat in the gate.

Abraham says, "My Lord." Lot says "My Lords."

Abraham had one Lord. Lot had "Lords many."

The men accepted Abraham's hospitality. They refused Lot's preferring the street.

Abraham's invitation accepted without pressure. Lot's only accepted after great pressure.

Abraham and Lot were of the same stock. They both lived in the same environment and were both righteous men. The contrast was the result of their respective choices during a crisis hour in each of their lives.

They are types of the spiritual (Abraham) and worldly believer (Lot).

Remember Lot's Wife

I. Remember her privileges
   Related to the people of God
   Faithfully instructed
   Warned of the danger

II. Remember her sin
   Presumption
   Unbelief
   Worldliness

III. Remember her fate
   Sudden
   Overwhelming
   Final

Beware of earthly entanglements.
Beware of questioning God's commands.
Beware of delays.
Beware of the backward look.

10

AN OLD TESTAMENT PICTURE OF CHRIST

"Where is the lamb?" Genesis 22:7.
"Behold the Lamb." John 1:29.

ISAAC

1. Isaac was promised.

    God told Abraham that he would give him a son and that through him all the families of the earth would be blessed.

2. Isaac's birth was supernatural.

    His father was too old. Abraham was past age and Sarah was past age. Sarah had never borne any children. Supernaturally Isaac was conceived and brought forth.

3. He was named before he was born.

4. The name Isaac means laughter (joy).

    There are two kinds of laughter and two kinds of joy. There is empty, giggling, noisy, boisterous laughter. Devils laugh like that. Then there is a holy laughter. There is a hilarity that comes as a result of holiness and that is a kind of joy that is meant here. When God told Sarah she was going to have a son she laughed; she thought it was impossible.

5. His own brother mocked him.

    Isaac was mild. Isaac was of a different nature to Ishmael. Ishmael was loud and boisterous. Isaac was just the opposite.

6. Isaac was offered up by his father as a sacrifice.

7. He carried the wood upon which he was to be offered.

8. The father and the son went together.
   That means they were one in offering; one in suffering; one in sacrifice; one in sorrow; one in self-denial. Abraham did not drag Isaac to the sacrifice. Abraham did not demand that Isaac go. They went together, hand in hand. They were one.

9. Isaac was submissive to his father's will.
   There are very few Isaacs living in the world today. Most of us want a little of our own will, but Isaac was submissive to his father's will.

10. Isaac was obedient to his father's word.
    All Abraham had to do was to say something and Isaac obeyed.

11. Isaac trusted to his father's goodness and love.
    He had absolute confidence in his father. He never doubted his father. He implicitly confided in his father Abraham. There wasn't a question in Isaac's mind but that his father was doing the very best for him. Isaac never doubted him. There wasn't a ripple in Isaac's soul or mind or heart about what his father was doing. He was an ideal son.

12. Isaac was a *willing* sacrifice.
    His father did not bind him before he put him on the wood. He stepped upon the wood himself and was bound. Isaac was at least 33

when this happened. He wasn't a child. He wasn't a little boy. His father didn't carry him there; it was three days' journey and he walked with his father. He could have resisted his father for the father was an old man. Isaac submitted.

13. After Isaac was offered he went home again.

14. After Isaac arrived home a servant was sent to obtain a bride for him.

15. The bride was to be related to his father (Abraham). Not a Canaanite or enemy.

16. Isaac was an heir to all his father's possessions.
    He was Abraham's only son by Sarah and Abraham gave him all he possessed.

17. Isaac received all his father's possessions.

18. Isaac stayed at home while the bride was sought and found.

19. Isaac waited patiently for his bride.

20. Isaac met his bride away from home.

21. Isaac took her to his father's house.

22. Isaac married her, loved her, and was comforted.
    Notice, it was after Sarah died. Sarah is a type of the Jews. When Christ and his bride meet in the air and they go to his father's house that will be the first time anyone has ever visited the father's house. The saints are not there yet; they are in Paradise. The wicked are in Hades or Hell.

Isaac is a beautiful picture of Christ. Christ was

promised . . . Born supernaturally . . . Named before
he was born . . . He means joy. (Salvation is always
followed by joy . . .) His brethren, too, mocked him.
He was offered up by his Father as a sacrifice. He
carried the wood, the Cross, upon His own shoulder,
upon which he was to die. The Father (God) and the
Son (Christ) went both of them together. Christ was
submissive to His Father's will. He, too, was obedient
to his Father's word. He, too, trusted to His Father's
goodness and love. Christ was a WILLING sacrifice.
After he was offered He, too, went back home. A servant (the Holy Spirit) was then sent to get Him a bride.
The Bride is a member of the Father's House, i. e. Born
Again Ones. Christ is also Heir to all. He also is now
at home, waiting now, patiently, for His Bride. Christ
also will meet His Bride away from His home, (i. e.
in the air). Christ will take His Bride for a honeymoon trip to his Father's House. *He* will be satisfied
and *she* will be satisfied. Who, but God, could have
put this picture in the Old Testament 2000 years before
Christ was born?

Isaac is thus one of the greatest types of our Lord
Jesus Christ found in the Bible. Promised before he
was born, despised and mocked by his own, left his
home and went on a long journey to a place of suffering and sacrifice. He carried the wood upon his own
shoulders upon which he was to be offered, and having been bound to the wood which he himself carried
was offered as a sacrifice to God. The Father and the
son suffered together and Isaac was submissive to the
will of his father. Not only was he obedient to the
will of his father, but he trusted implicitly in his father's
goodness and love and became a willing sacrifice. After
being offered as a sacrifice he returned home, and after

he arrived home the servant was sent to obtain for him a bride.

Isaac remained home until the bride was obtained and he became heir of all of the father's possessions and finally met his bride in the open field, took her to his father's house and Isaac was happy and comforted. What a picture of a greater than Isaac, even our Lord Jesus Christ! He was promised and named before He was born, despised and mocked, left His home and started on a long journey to a place of suffering and sacrifice, carried the wood upon His own shoulders upon which He was to be offered, submissive to the will of His Father as well as to the Father's word, trusting implicitly in His Father's goodness and love became a willing sacrifice, wholly acceptable unto God. After He was offered as a sacrifice He returned home and upon arriving sent His servant, the Holy Spirit, to obtain for Himself a bride. He will remain home until the bride is obtained. The Holy Spirit is even now seeking out the bride of Christ. Having become heir of all His Father's possessions, He awaits the bride. He will meet her in the open field for we "shall be caught up together with them in the clouds, to meet the Lord in the air and so shall we ever be with the Lord." We shall be forever with our happy Bridegroom. He shall take His bride to the Father's many mansioned home over there. This will constitute the honeymoon trip of the bridegroom (Christ) and His bride. Christ will thus "see the travail of His soul, and shall be satisfied."

11

THE BRIDE OF CHRIST

"Wilt thou go?"
"I will go." Genesis 24: 58.

Israel was the Old Testament Bride or Wife of Jehovah. Israel went into adultery and was consequently divorced. Adultery is the only spiritual ground for divorce and since Israel proved unfaithful she was put away. The new Bride is the Lamb's wife. There are eight brides mentioned in the Bible the first of whom was Eve and the second Rebekah. Rebekah is a very beautiful type of the Bride of Christ. All the characters and events of the Old Testament seem to be strikingly typical of the events of the future. Coming events were casting their shadows before. Adam was a type of Christ as the perfect, holy, pure, sinless one. Eve was a type of the Bride of Christ sharing with Adam in the dominion of the Earth. Isaac was also a type of Christ and Rebekah is a type of the Bride of Christ.

Rebekah is found at a well. She is at the well to draw sparkling, nourishing, refreshing water both for herself and for others. She is not found at the movies or on the dance floor or in the theatre. She is found at a well. She is not found reading the yellow back, or blue back, novels or novelettes; she is found at a well. It is a very suggestive and remarkable fact that both Isaac and Jacob, as well as Moses, found their brides at a well. Rebekah was found at a well. This is the first qualification for the bridehood saints. They must know how to draw water both for themselves and for others. The bridehood saints are not only saved and sanctified, but they are busy drawing water out of the wells of salvation for themselves and for others.

Again, Rebekah was a virgin and fair, pleasant and beautiful. Only such are found among the bridehood saints. If we would qualify as members of the bridehood saints we must be spiritually clean, chaste, pure, pleasant and beautiful.

Again, Rebekah was a willing, earnest, zealous, untiring worker for others. She was ready and willing to draw water and satisfy the need of ten camels.

Ten in the Bible is the number of completeness. One is the number for God and there cannot be any other numbers without beginning with the number one.

Two is the number for man and it is a very remarkable fact that Christ is said to be the second man. All other men have been and are wrecks and derelicts on the sea of life. Adam was the first and Christ was the second man. We have never seen a man as God created him.

Three is the number for the Trinity. God, the Father, God, the Son, and God, the Holy Spirit. Man is a Trinity, spirit, soul and body. God made man (soul and body) and then breathed into him the breath of life (spirit) and man became a living soul.

Four is the number for the world of mankind.

Five is the number of grace and six is the number of evil.

Six six six (666) is the number of the Anti-christ and points out the trinity of evil, the climax of wickedness.

Seven is the number of perfection; eight is the

number of that which is NEW and ten is the number of completeness. We have the parables of the ten virgins, the ten pounds and the ten talents. Jacob's wages were changed ten times and in the lesson before us there were ten camels. Camels are desert travelers. They are travelers across the thirsty desert. They can take in sufficient water to supply their needs for weeks at a time if necessary. Rebekah was ready and willing to completely give herself to suffer, serve and sacrifice in order to satisfy the thirst of weary travelers across a thirsty desert. This was quite a backbreaking, limb-tiring job, but she set herself to work and worked with zest and accomplished the task with joy.

Rebekah was an untiring worker on behalf of others. There was not a lazy bone in her body; there was not a drop of careless, indifferent lethargic blood in her veins. No wonder she became the happy bride of the loving Isaac.

> Go labor on, spend and be spent
>   Thy joy to do the Master's will;
> It is the way the Master went,
>   Should not the servant tread it still?
>
> Toil on and in thy toil rejoice
>   For toil comes rest, for exile home
> Soon shalt thou hear the Bridegroom's voice,
>   The mid-night cry, behold I come.

With only a small pitcher with which to draw water, and in many cases the well was deep, it must, therefore, have taken quite a time to satisfy the need of ten camels. But Rebekah stuck to the job until it was finished. Without a word of encouragement from anyone she gladly fulfilled her appointed task; thus satisfying the need of thirsty desert travelers who otherwise would have perished by the way.

Men die in darkness at your side
  Without a hope to cheer the tomb,
Take up the torch and wave it wide,
  The torch that lights time's thickest gloom.

Go labor on,'tis not for nought
  Thy earthly loss is heavenly gain,
Men heed thee, love thee, praise thee NOT,
  The Master praises! what are men?

Not until each and all of the ten camels were satisfied, not until the thirst of these desert travelers was quenched, not until she had hasted and ran to the well and ran and hasted to the trough, not until the task was performed and the job was done did Rebekah receive a word of encouragement from Eliezer. How different it is today with most would be Rebekahs. If the pastor or some one else is not everlastingly running around with a milk bottle or a honey jar, the most of the professing Rebekahs today will neither draw water for themselves nor for others. They seem to be in everlasting need of soothing syrup. Many a good pastor is distracted, taking crutches around for the cripples, carrying milk for the babies and honey for the soured in order to keep his flock together and encouraged. These would-be Rebekahs take offense at the least thing and up the miff-tree they go and still keep up their miserable profession.

But again, Rebekah was a faithful witness as well as a willing worker. She returned to her home and testified to all in the house, relating to them her happy experience. She was ready to go with Eliezer, take the lonely way across a trackless desert with a hot sun above her head and burning sand beneath her feet. She was ready for every sand storm, every pain, every ache, every test, every trial and every tear that may be necessary in order to finish her course with joy and at last be the happy bride of Isaac. She was ready to press her way through every obstacle, suffer any and every discomfort, and mind the voice of the faithful servant in order to be the honored bride of the loving Isaac. If we ever hope to be amongst the bridehood saints, we must not only draw water from the wells of salvation and give the water of life to others and work on untiringly and even without encouragement from anyone around, but we must witness to others, be prepared for every storm that we may meet, be willing to bear every pain, endure every test that may be necessary, press our way through every obstacle, mind the voice of the Spirit, go where He wants us to go and do what He wants us to do.

Rebekah was at last fully and completely rewarded. The journey was finished, the storms were over and all behind her. She alighted from the camel's back and was presented to her lovely bridegroom and

> Safe in the arms of Isaac,
>   Safe on his gentle breast,
> There by his love overshadowed
>   Sweetly did Rebekah rest.

12

JACOB

"Therefore God give thee of the dew of heaven, and the fatness of the earth, and plenty of corn and wine: Let people serve thee, and nations bow down to thee: be lord over thy brethren, and let thy mother's sons bow down to thee: cursed be every one that curseth thee and blessed be he that blesseth thee." **Genesis 27: 28-29.**

There are two sides to Jacob's character:
1. Things *against* him.
2. Thinks for *him.*
1. Things against Jacob
    a. *Before* his birth he struggled.
    b. *At* his birth he grasps.
    c. *After* his birth he cheats and lies.
       Jacob obtained the birthright and blessing by fraud. It belonged to Esau, but God wanted Jacob to have it and God had a plan and purpose in order to give it to Jacob.
       Jacob wasted twenty years of his life as a wanderer, a fugitive, toiling, suffering and in a strange land. That was because he did not wait God's time. If Jacob had waited God's time he would not have had to wait twenty years. He wasted twenty years of what might have been a useful life and all the time he was being cheated. He had cheated and now he was being cheated. His wages were changed ten times. He served seven years for Rachel and then served seven years more. After that

he served six more years, making twenty years in all. Jacob was completely beaten, completely defrauded. His own sin found him out.

2. Things for Jacob

a. Jacob was God's choice. He was elected of God. Before he was born and while he was being born and after he was born he was God's favorite.

b. Jacob valued God's blessing.

c. Jacob valued God's promises.

d. He lived for the future.

> The birthright meant God's blessing. The birthright meant that whoever had it would inherit God's promises. The birthright meant something away off in the future that the one who had it would obtain and Jacob wanted that blessing. He coveted God's blessing. He went about it in a wrong way, but he was right in what he was after. He was after God's blessing. He craved, coveted, longed for, and made up his mind to get the blessing of God. Do you crave God's blessing? Esau thought very lightly of it. Esau was indifferent to God's blessing. A bowl of soup was more to Esau than something out in the future. But Jacob was master over his own stomach and he surrendered his stomach and his soup in order to get the birthright. Go after God's blessing. Be warned about going after it in the wrong way.

> Jacob wanted the promises even though he

went about it in the wrong way. (God doesn't excuse him for doing it; God never said "Amen" to his cheating; God never said "Amen" to his lies.) Jacob lived in view of the future. The birthright had nothing in the present. It was all in the future and so Jacob closed his eyes to the present and he looked out into the future and he planned to get future blessing. His gaze was afar off; he was dreaming. You will never accomplish anything for God or man unless you dream things. Never be afraid to be called a dreamer.

Now you see the contrast between Jacob and Esau. Esau was out hunting and stayed so long he forgot he was hungry and then he became so hungry he couldn't wait five minutes for a meal to be cooked for him. He looked on his brother's bowl of soup and wanted it. Esau was like that. He was willing to sell God's blessings. He was willing to sell God's favor, willing to give up all God's promises and willing to sacrifice the whole future for a basin of broth. Judas sold Christ for thirty pieces of silver. Esau sold his birthright, and that included Jesus Christ, for a basin of broth. Jacob wanted God's blessing. Do you? He looked out into the future. Are you? Or are you looking merely to the things of time and sense?

e. God favors him with a dream (Bethel) (Conversion). Bethel means the house of God. "El" in the Bible is the word used for

God. Beth means house. Beth-el, house of God. That speaks of Jacob's conversion.

f. Jacob begins to tithe.

That is a very important point in Jacob's life. Jacob lived four hundred years before Moses; Jacob lived four hundred years before the law; so you see the tithe is not Law. It was four hundred years before the law. Abraham was Jacob's grandfather and Jacob's grandfather tithed and he lived five hundred years before Moses. Five hundred years before the Law, Abraham tithed. Four hundred years before the Law, Jacob tithed, and so the tithe is not Law. It is not the Mosaic Law. Tithing is not bringing anything under Law. It was before the Law; it remained after the Law. Jacob was dishonest in many things, but he was honest enough to pay his tithes. The tithe is an acknowledgement that everything belongs to God. If we keep back the tithe we tell God it is ours and that nothing we have belongs to Him.

Jacob was grasping, but not nearly as grasping as some folk. Heathen nations tithe and they have done it ever since Shem, Ham and Japheth came out of the ark. "These things ought ye to do," said Jesus, "and not to leave the other undone."

g. God protects and preserves him.

Esau was mad and Jacob feared his brother Esau. If you do wrong to anybody you can't meet them as you ought to meet them. Jacob had done things against Esau and now he was afraid to meet his brother. God gives him courage and God turns the whole thing around so that they become friends.

h. Jacob received a second crisis or blessing.

First crisis, Bethel (justification). Second crisis, Peniel (sanctification). Bethel speaks of his conversion. Peniel speaks of his sanctification. Bethel means the house of God. Peniel means the face of God. Peni means face; el means God.

First, Bethel, i. e., he gets into God's household, is born again, and then he sees the face of God and that is purity of heart. Jacob has two crises and there are about twenty years between them. The first was at Bethel; then he comes to Peniel. Notice, it says the angel wrestled with Jacob; not Jacob wrestled with the angel. Jacob was so warped and twisted the angel could not do anything with him. That angel is a type of Jesus Christ. Jacob's thigh was broken and he went away limping. His strength was broken; his will was broken; his thigh was broken; he was helpless, and helpless he fell into the arms of Christ.

i. Jacob's name was changed.

Jacob, the rascal; Jacob, the scoundrel; Jacob, the man before the new birth. He is also spoken of as Jacob and Israel. That speaks of the new man and old man together. Jacob, the natural man and Israel, the new man. Jacob is the fleshly man and Israel, the spiritual man. Then Jacob was killed and nothing left but Israel. He became "Prince with God." The old nature was gone. The name Jacob by itself speaks of the natural man; man by nature, a sinner.

Jacob and Israel speaks of the justified, but not sanctified Jacob; the old nature and the new nature; the Old Man and the Holy Spirit; Isaac and Ishmael in the same house. Israel by itself speaks of the entirely sanctified man.

Jacob, the scheming sinner, was changed to Israel, the sanctified saint.

There is great significance attached to Bible names and the changing of them. The name of the first woman was Adam, and it was not until *after* the temptation and fall that her name was *changed* to Eve.

The name of Abram was changed to Abraham. Abram means High father with the emphasis upon the *high*. Abraham means the father of a multitude, and thus THE HIGH was taken out of Abram.

The name Sarai was changed to Sarah and thus the little i was taken out of Sarah. Abraham lost the big high and Sarah lost the little i, which excuses itself from doing anything, because it cannot do everything.

Adam means "red earth" and Eve means mother, "the mother of the living one" which points forward to Christ.

Saul of Tarsus was changed to Paul, and therein we have the secret of Paul's great usefulness. The word Saul means *big*, whereas the word Paul means *little*. How

different it was with the Saul of the Old
Testament. His name was not changed.

JACOB AS A TYPE OF ISRAEL

1. His name was changed from Jacob to Israel.

   Adam was a type of Christ as the second man.
   Abel was a type of Christ as the innocent sufferer. Noah was a type of the saints who go
   up during the period of the Great Tribulation.
   (He went through the floods and came back
   after they were over, and he stands for the Jews
   during the Great Tribulation.) Enoch was a
   type of the translated saints at the close of this
   dispensation. Enoch never died. Moses died and
   Elijah is coming back to die, but Enoch will
   never die. He is a type of the rapture of the
   church, going up without dying. Abraham is a
   type of the man of faith, the believer. Everything he did was by faith. Isaac typifies son-
   ship. Jacob is the typical servant. Joseph is
   the typical ruler. Take them all separately and
   they are all typical of different things. Put them
   together and they are typical again. Rebekah
   is the typical bride; Jacob was a type of the
   Israelites. His name was changed to Israel.

2. He was the object of God's election.

   He was elected by God; chosen by God; fore-
   ordained by God; he obtained the birthright;
   was to have possession of Canaan. He was an
   object of God's electing grace. The children of
   Israel were objects of God's electing grace. He
   chose them and delivered them from Egypt.

3. He was loved before he was born.

   You remember the Lord said in connection with

Israel, "I have loved thee with an everlasting love." Israel, like Isaac, and Jacob, like Israel, were loved before they were born.

4. Jacob had no natural attractiveness.

There was nothing about him to merit God's favor, smile or approval. Think of the things that were against him: Grasping, struggling, cheating, lying and defrauding. He was so warped and twisted no one else but God would have chosen him. The same was true of Israel.

5. God gave him the earthly inheritance.

Palestine belongs to Israel. Jacob was promised Palestine and Israel is promised Palestine. Palestine belonged to Jacob by virtue of his being loved before he was born and by virtue of his obtaining the birthright.

6. Jacob was exiled from Canaan as a result of sin.

He was compelled to leave home (Canaan, Palestine). Why is it that the Jews are not in Palestine today? Because of their sin. What sin was it that settled their doom? Rejection of Christ.

7. Jacob was a wanderer outside of Palestine.

For twenty years he was a wanderer, a fugitive and a vagabond away from his own land. The Jews now are the people of the wandering foot. They don't settle anywhere. They are men and women of wandering feet.

8. He was sorely chastened by God.

He tasted the bitter pill of sorrow and suffering because of his disobedience. That is exactly what Israel is doing now. The Jews are suffering now.

9. Jacob longed to get back again to Palestine.
   The Jews are longing to get back to Palestine.

10. He was unjustly treated in the land of exile.
    Outside of this land of America and England the Jews have been murdered and killed almost everywhere since 70 A.D. For 1850 years, because of their sin and disobedience, they have been unjustly treated. Russia has murdered thousands of them. Europe has shed the blood of thousands. That assures us that England and America will go through the millennium, because of their treatment of the Jews. Those nations which have treated the Jews properly will go through the millennium and be judged after the Millennium. (Matthew 25: 31-46.)

11. He became a crafty schemer.
    How he schemed. How crafty he was. A perfect picture of the Jews today.

12. Jacob used subtle devices to get rich.
    He had cunning ways in order to get rich. A perfect picture of the Jews today.

13. God promised to bring him back again to his own land.
    Twenty years was a long time, but God had promised. It seemed as though Jacob would die outside of Canaan, but God has promised to bring him back. Just so, Israel.

14. Jacob received no further revelation from God during all the years he was in exile.
    Has Israel received any revelation from God during the last eighteen hundred fifty years? No. God has not dealt with Israel for eighteen

hundred fifty years. He is dealing with this world now. They have never received any revelation since the year 70 A. D.

15. Jacob was marvelously preserved in a strange land. If you want a proof as to the inspiration of the Bible you have it in one word, namely Israel. Every other nation that has ever lived has risen and gone and is no more. The greatest nations with teeming millions of people have gone. Where is Babylon? They lived before the Jews, but they are gone. Where is the Medo-Persian Empire? Where is the Roman Empire with all its Caesars and Neros? You can no more kill off the Jews than you can kill the Bible. The world has tried and tried over and over again to destroy the Bible, but they cannot do it. So the world has tried to kill off the Jews, but they cannot do it. You can't burn them out. You can't starve them out. You can't kill them out. Here is a standing proof that God lives and the Bible is true. Whenever you see a Jew you may think of him as standing evidence of the truth of the Word of God. Neither the Jew nor the Bible can be destroyed.

16. Jacob became very wealthy while in exile. Are the Jews wealthy? They are in a strange land and they are amassing enormous wealth everywhere in the world. They are the greatest money-getters in the world. The second richest man in the world, Rothschild, has governed the British Empire with his money. He is a Jew. He almost had the world in his grasp. The British and French governments could not have carried on the World War I if it had not been

for Rothschild and those like him with their millions.

17. Jacob ultimately returned to Palestine with the wealth of the Gentiles.
Israel shall yet return to Palestine with the wealth of the Gentiles.

18. Jacob blesses the Gentiles.
This was almost the last act in Jacob's life. He stretched out his hands to Heaven, and he blessed his own sons, and then he blessed the Gentiles; Pharaoh; Egypt. That is exactly what the Jews shall do in the future. Through Israel, blessing is coming to the world.

Notice, Abraham was promised two kinds of seed. First, he was promised seed as the sand of the seashore for multitude. (Earthly Israel, the Jews.) Second, he was promised seed as the stars of Heaven for multitude. (The Heavenly people.) One is the earthly people, the sand, (Israel). The other is the Heavenly people, (the church and the bride). Then God spake to him the third time and the thing is turned right around and the stars are mentioned first. The church is now first. Wonderful prophecy! Marvelous Word! Wonderful Book of God!

There is a difference between Israel and the Jews. It is plain in Genesis. The first Hebrew was Abraham. The first Jew was Judah. The first Israelite was Jacob. The Israelites lived long before the Jews and the Israelites and the Jews are not the same. God knows where they are and he is going to bring them out some day. There may be a little Israelite blood mixed with some of the Jews, but they are not real Israelites. We know what a Jew looks like, but we do not know what an Israelite looks like.

There are pictures, types, shadows, emblems, foreshadowings in the Book of Genesis that ought to convince anybody of the truth of the Word of God. *Only* God could have put them there. Joseph was almost a perfect picture of CHRIST, and Jacob was almost a perfect picture of Israel.

JACOB'S LADDER

"And he saith unto him, verily, verily, I say unto you, Hereafter ye shall see heaven open, and the angels of God ascending and descending upon the Son of Man." John 1: 51.

1. An original way .... Heb. 10:20
2. An open way .... Heb. 9:26
3. A God given way .... Isa. 35:8-9
4. An only way .... John 14:6
5. A satisfactory way

> Jacob's ladder was not only an original way and an open way, but it was complete. It linked heaven and earth together.

THE VISION OF JACOB

Genesis 28:10-22

At nits-end corner God steps in as illustrated by three Hebrew children—Daniel—Stephen—John—Jacob. Notice:

1. The sinners' plight
   ". . . night . . . sun had set"
   ". . . a certain place . . ."

2. The way to heaven made plain
    ". . . a ladder . . . CHRIST"
    ". . . the Angels of God"
3. God reveals Himself
    ". . . the Lord stood above it . . ."
    Through the ladder God became visible
    to Jacob.
    Here is the Gospel according to Jacob.
    Canaan is promised.
    Protection is assured.
4. Jacob is converted.
    "This is the house of God."
    God dwells in Christ.
    "This is the gate of Heaven."
    Christ is the Door.
5. The Proof of his conversion.
    1. The anointed Pillar of Praise.
    2. The Vow of Consecration.

THE SANCTIFICATION OF JACOB

Genesis 32: 24-31

Notice:

1. The Consternation of Jacob.
    ". . . afraid and distressed"
2. The Crippling of Jacob.
    "He touched . . . out of joint"
3. The Changing of Jacob.
    ". . . Israel . . ."
    Compare Eve
        Abram
        Sarah
        Paul
4. The Clinging of Jacob.
    ". . . . I will not let thee go . . ."

5. The Confession of Jacob.
   "I am Jacob"
   "I have seen God . . ."
   Testimony . . . Witnessing

Observe:
1. His walk proved he had the blessing.
2. After he got the blessing it says
   "THE SUN AROSE UPON HIM."

POWER WITH GOD AND MAN

Genesis 32: 28-29

When Jacob prevailed with God he also prevailed with man.

I. What it is NOT:
   1. Not Physical Power
   2. Not Mental Power
   3. Not Magical Power
   4. Not Demon Power
   5. Not Independent Power

II. What it is:
   1. God's Power
   2. Spiritual Power
   3. Miracle working Power
   4. Power to Witness
   5. Power to Win

III. What it does: "And he blessed him there"
   1. Saves from great peril.
      Esau had threatened to kill him.
   2. Heals wounds.
      "Esau kissed him"
   3. Transforms.
      Jacob to Israel

Prevailing Prayer

1. Abraham for a Son
2. Abraham for Sodom
3. Moses for Pharaoh
4. Moses against Amalek
5. Moses for Israel
6. Hannah for a son
7. David for forgiveness
8. Hezekiah for healing
9. Jonah for deliverance
10. Apostles for Pentecost

> In each case there came a moment when struggling ceased and heart faith was exercised.

Jacob received the blessing when he ceased struggling.

Prevailing Prayer in Genesis

1. *Abel* brought of the firstlings of the flock. He provided a lamb. He slew the lamb, spilled its blood, presented it to God, and waited for God's acceptance. He thus acknowledged his own need, pleaded the blood of an innocent victim, waited until the fire fell and the witness was borne to his own heart that he was righteous. Abel shows us the way through to God. He received the witness that he was righteous.

2. *Abraham* took an heifer three years old, a she goat three years old, a ram three years old, a turtle dove and a young pigeon. He divided them in the midst, laid each piece one against another, and offered them to God. While waiting for God's acceptance the fowls came down and Abraham drove them away. Driving away the fowls was tiring work and sunset found Abraham weary, worn and sleepy. The sun disappeared over the western hills and an horror of great darkness fell upon Abraham. He kept the night watch, however, and waited until, behold,

there came a smoking furnace and a lamp of fire, and with them came the witness of Abraham that God was pleased.

The Heifer typifies Christ as the
> Suffering
> Sacrificing
> Servant of God and man.

Three years old, sets forth the truth that after three years of service Christ would be offered.

The GOAT typifies Christ who was made a curse for us. The curse was only one of the many consequences of the fall of man and Christ became a curse, for cursed is every one that hangeth on a tree.

The FEMALE goat speaks of the tenderness and fruitfulness of Christ who has the affection, love, tenderness and sympathy of the woman as well as the strength and energy of the man.

The RAM typifies Christ as the separated, consecrated substitute dying in our stead.
> As the ram was a substitute for Isaac, so Christ is our Substitute.

The DOVE typifies Christ as the heavenly one come down to earth to suffer and die. The gentle, harmless, winsome, wooing affection of the dove is perfectly exhibited in Jesus Christ.

The DIVIDING of these offerings sets forth the sufferings of Christ as he gave his soul an offering for sin.

Abraham thus pleaded the merits of Christ, who was God's patient suffering servant. He pleaded the blood of Christ as the one who became a curse for us. He pleaded the efficacy of the heavenly one who, in humiliation, came down and offered himself without spot to God.

The FOWLS typify the multiplied forces of evil arrayed against all those who would hear from heaven. We must fight the good fight of faith against all the powers of darkness and tenaciously hold on in prayer until God answers.

The DARKNESS typifies the last stage through which the believer must plow if he ever hears from heaven. We must plead the blood, hold on by persistent, believing prayer and in due time heaven will answer and our need shall be supplied.

3. *Jacob* was converted at Bethel (House of God) and sanctified wholly at Peniel (Face of God) for "blessed are the pure in heart for they shall see God."

Jacob's bent to evil was destroyed by the omnipotent touch of Christ. His name was changed to Israel (Prince of God) and this sets forth the transformation of Jacob the supplanter to a Prevailing Prince. The Angel (Christ) descended, laid hold upon Jacob, and wrestled him to the count, and put his thigh out of joint. Jacob, thus made *completely helpless* and *dependent,* could only CLING, and clinging, he refused to be denied, prevailed with Christ, and was blessed. Thus Genesis teaches us how to pray and prevail with God.

"The Book of Genesis is the seed in which the plant of God's Word is enfolded. It is the starting point of God's gradually-unfolding plan of the ages. Genesis is the plinth of the pillar of the Divine revelation. It is the root of the tree of the inspired Scriptures. It is the source of the stream of the holy writings of the Bible. If the base of the pillar is removed, the pillar falls. If the root of the tree is cut out, the tree will wither and die. If the fountain head of the stream is cut off, the stream will dry up. The Bible as a whole is like a chain hanging upon two staples. The Book of Genesis is the one staple; the Book of Revelation is the other. Take away either staple, the chain falls in confusion. If the first chapters of Genesis are unreliable, the revelation of the beginning of the universe, the origin of the race, and the reason of its redemption are gone. If the last chapters of Revelation are displaced the consummation of all things is unknown. If you take away Genesis, you have lost the explanation of the first heaven, the first earth, the first Adam, and the fall. If you take away Revelation you have lost the completed truth of the new heaven, and the new earth, man redeemed, and the second Adam in Paradise regained."

"And Esau wept." Genesis 27:28.

1. Esau was a cunning hunter.

> He was a man who loved the open doors and his greatest pleasure, like a goodly number of people today, were in hunting and fishing. He was a pleasure-hunting man. He was a man of the field. Jesus says, "the field is the world," so Esau was a man of the world.
>
> After he had been out all day hunting in the field he came home *hungry*. He came home *dissatisfied* and that speaks of people who do their best to get pleasure out of this world (the field) and then they are still dissatisfied. After they have done their best there is still an aching void within. Jacob was a plain man. Esau was a rough man of the field. Jacob lived in a tent. Esau wasn't satisfied with that kind of life.

2. Esau gave up the future for the present.

> Esau had the birthright. The birthright meant future blessing. Esau had it. Esau could have inherited future blessing, but for a bowl of broth he gave up future prospects and future blessings. He surrendered the future for the present. He surrendered his soul for his body. He surrendered the things of heaven for the things of earth.

3. Esau placed no value on the things of God.

> Very few people have the right conception as

to what the birthright meant. The birthright meant God's favor. The birthright meant God's blessing. The birthright meant future happiness. The birthright meant all the land of Canaan belonged to him and he surrendered it all for one square meal. He gave up God's favor for a basin of hot soup. He gave up God's blessing to satisfy his stomach. There are a lot of people who come up against holiness and refuse to go into the land of Canaan because of their stomach; because of their home. They would rather have something in the present, something tangible now, than the blessing of God in the present or future. The best things, so far as we are concerned, are in the future. Esau was a man who placed no value on the things of God. There are a lot of people just like that today. They don't want God's blessing. They don't want God's favor. They would rather have a big house. They would rather have a little pleasure down here, something tangible here, than heaven hereafter.

4. Esau despised and sold the birthright.

That means he sold the favor of God. That means that he sold the love and blessing of God. That means that he despised being God's man. *All that* is included in despising his birthright. In a word, he despised God and holiness. That birthright meant God above him pouring his blessing upon him. Esau says, "I don't care whether God is above me or not, I don't want His blessing." The birthright means that God's favor and kindness is around the man who possesses it. God is pledged to protect that man.

Esau says, "I don't care for God's favor; I don't care for God's protection; I don't care for God's blessing." That is what it means to despise the birthright. Canaan is the type of holiness and when Esau despised Canaan, that is the picture of a man despising holiness.

5. Esau regretted when it was too late.

After he had partaken of his basin of broth and found the birthright gone he begins to bawl; he begins to cry; he wants it back again, but it is *too late*. Jacob has it. He wept bitterly and cried, "Oh God, give me that blessing," but there was no answer.

There are men and women today who would do anything to get God's blessing. They repent when it is too late. Esau repented when it was too late. The first lesson that we ought to learn here: Value God's blessing. Value the favor of God. Another lesson: Surrender the things of earth for the things of Heaven. Give up the soap-bubbles of life, the gold and glitter of time and make yourself a home in the city of God. Esau was a fool. I wonder what he thinks of his choice now?

Esau

1. A man of uncontrolled passions.
2. A man exercising little self-restraint.
3. A man of swift impulses.
4. Careless and reckless of consequences.
5. Without any heart for God.
6. Without any soul for spiritual things.
7. A rebel against the law of God.

8. Wrongly married (he married a colored woman).
9. Supplanted himself and was in turn supplanted.
10. A profane person, repenting when too late.

OVERDRIVING THE YOUNG

Genesis 33:13

I. How we may overdrive:
   1. By puzzling points of doctrine.
   2. By condemning their opinions.
   3. By erecting a too high standard.
   4. By preaching nothing but the severer truths of the Bible.
   5. By austerity of manner, harshness.
   6. By fault finding and never commending.
   7. Dwelling constantly upon the trials and temptations of the Christian life.

II. Remember:
   1. Our own experience when young.
   2. Others must still bear with us.
   3. The Holy Spirit dwells in all God's Children.
   4. Kill the lambs this year; what about the sheep next year?
   5. The tenderness of Jesus.

14

JOSEPH

"JOSEPH is yet alive." Genesis 45:26.

The book of Genesis sets forth in glowing terms the life, character and conduct of this most remarkable man.

1. The name Joseph means "increase" or "to add."
2. He was a shepherd.
3. He was a willing and obedient servant.
4. Especially loved by his father.
5. Greatly honored.
   He was given a coat of many colors, and this was a special mark of favor.
6. Hated by his own brethren.
7. Hated without a cause.
8. A prophet of his own coming glory.
   He dreamed that the sun, moon and stars bowed down to him.
   The sun typifies his father, while the moon typified his mother and the stars typified his brethren, who would bow down to him. He was thus a prophet of his own coming exaltation.
9. He witnessed to his brethren.
10. The more he witnessed, the more they hated him.
11. He was envied and slandered.
12. He was sent on a mission of love to his brethren.
    His brethren had been away from home a long time. The father became concerned for them and sent Joseph to seek the welfare of his brethren.

115

13. Joseph was ready and willing to go.

> "Here I am," he said to the father. If it means suffering, sacrifice, long separation from home, Amen. "Thy will, my father, be done."

14. He left home to seek his brethren.

> No matter how long and how dreary the road, Joseph was ready and willing to seek his brethren.

15. While seeking his brethren he had no place in which to sleep.

> Joseph slept under the open canopy of heaven. Without having a place wherein to stay. Having no place to lay his head. He, nevertheless, loved his brethren and sought their welfare.

16. His brethren conspired against him.

17. They decided to kill him.

18. Joseph is stripped of his raiment.

19. His brethren cause him untold sorrow and suffering.

20. Joseph is *sold* for twenty pieces of *silver*.

21. His brethren deliver him to his enemies.

22. While Joseph was suffering, they sat down to eat bread.

> While Jesus was on the cross the Jews, his brethren, partook of the passover supper.

23. Jacob (Israel) thought he was dead.

24. Rejected by his own, he served the Egyptians.

25. Severely tested, falsely accused, he maintained his integrity.

26. While suffering for righteousness sake, he preached to two prisoners.

27. Everything came to pass as Joseph had said.

28. After suffering innocently, he was exalted to a throne.

29. All people were compelled to bow the knee to Joseph.

30. Joseph received a new name.

> This new name was Zaphnath-Paaneah, which means "the revealer of secrets." Joseph was not only a savior, but he became the revealer of secrets. This shall be the new name of Jesus. He shall become the eternal revealer of secrets to his chosen bride.

31. Joseph married a Gentile bride.

32. Joseph and his bride rule and reign together.
    1. Rejected by his own
    2. Suffered innocently
    3. Exalted
    4. Marriage
    5. Rule

33. Joseph had all things at his disposal.

34. Reconciled to his brethren.

35. Supplied the needs of the world.

36. Ruled over all.

Here is a complete picture of our Lord Jesus Christ. Here is a life of Christ pre-written in detail setting forth both the sufferings and the glory of Christ.

Joseph is thus almost a perfect foreshadowing of our Lord Jesus Christ. The son of his father's love and especially honored by his father, a servant and a shepherd, hated without a cause, he became a prophet of his own coming glory. He witnessed to his brethren and the more he witnessed the more they hated him. He left his happy home to seek his own brethren and, while seeking his brethren, a stranger found him in the field without a place in which to sleep, not having where to lay his head. He sought his brethren and they conspired against him, stripped him of his raiment and sold him for twenty pieces of silver. Not only did he suffer innocently, but he was betrayed and his own brethren sat down to eat bread while he was suffering. Jacob thought he was dead, and although falsely accused and a servant to the Gentiles he maintained his integrity. He preached to the prisoners while he himself suffered. His feet were bound by fetters, and everything came to pass just as he had prophesied. Despised and rejected by his own, he was at last exalted to a throne, received a new name and married a Gentile bride. What a picture of a greater Joseph, even our Lord Jesus Christ.

He too was especially loved by His Father, became a servant and a shepherd, even the good, great and chief shepherd. He too was hated and hated without cause. He too was a prophet of His own coming glory and witnessed to His brethren. The more He witnessed the more He was hated. He too left His home to seek out His brethren. While seeking them, and before He found them, a stranger (the Gentiles) discovered Him in the field (the world). He suffered, was stripped of His raiment and sold for thirty pieces of silver, the price of a man slave as twenty pieces of silver was the price of a slave boy. He suffered until at last He was betrayed, and while suffering His brethren sat down to eat bread, for it was the Passover. Israel even now thinks that He is dead, but He is alive again and now is serving the Gentiles. And, although the fetters bound His feet, He now is exalted to a throne of grace and in a coming day will be exalted to a throne of glory and everything shall yet come to pass as He prophesied. He too has received a new name, and He too shall yet marry a Gentile bride. May we be accounted worthy to be one member of His glorious bride.

As all bowed their knees to Joseph, and as all things

were placed in his hands, and as he was at last reconciled to his own brethren, so all must bow the knee to Christ for all things are in His hands and He will yet be reconciled to His brethren, the Jews. As Joseph had the keys of the storehouse and supplied bread for all and saved all Egypt from death, so Christ has the keys to the Father's storehouse and He even now has bread enough to spare. He is the Bread of Life. If we need bread, we must go to Jesus as the world in Joseph's day went to Joseph.

Joseph was a revealer of secrets and the savior of the world.

Joseph was one of the seven representative men in the book of Genesis.

1. Adam, or God's ideal man.
2. Abel, the innocent sufferer.
3. Noah, the preacher of righteousness.
4. Melchisedek, the appointed priest of the Most High.
5. Isaac, the well beloved son.
6. Jacob the servant.
7. Joseph, the ruler.

In these seven representative men we have a perfect picture of *the man* Christ Jesus (Adam), of the Innocent Sufferer (Abel), of the faithful Preacher of Righteousness (Noah), of the true Melchisedek, of the well beloved Son (Isaac), of the Royal Servant (Jacob), and of the coming Ruler, who will save the world from death (Joseph).

1. Adam and Eve, who set forth Christ and His bride.
2. Cain and Abel, who set forth salvation by works and salvation by faith.
3. Enoch and Noah, who set forth the heavenly saints and the earthly saints.

4. Abraham and Lot, who set forth the walk by faith and the walk by sight.
5. Isaac and Ishmael, who set forth the life of the Spirit and the walk after the flesh.
6. Esau and Jacob, who illustrate the natural man and the spiritual man.
7. Joseph with his brethren, who foreshadow Christ and the children of Israel.

FAITH IN THE BOOK OF GENESIS

1. Abel .... Justifying Faith
2. Enoch .... Sanctifying Faith
3. Noah .... Working Faith
4. Abraham .... Separating Faith
5. Isaac .... Patient Faith
6. Jacob .... Suffering Faith
7. Joseph .... Victorious Faith

"The first book of the Bible is for several reasons one of the most interesting and fascinating portions of Scripture. Its place in the Canon, its relation to the rest of the Bible, and the varied and striking character of its contents combine to make it one of the most prominent in Holy Writ. It is with a real spiritual insight, therefore, that the people of God in all ages have fastened upon this book, and given it their earnest attention. It is also a testimony to its value and importance that criticism of various kinds and degrees has also concentrated itself upon this first book of the Bible. Its substance and claim are far too important to be overlooked."

Dr. W. A. Griffith Thomas
(Devotional Commentary, p. 1)

15

THE TWELVE SONS OF JACOB

All names of the Bible and all changes of names in the Bible have a present, a practical, as well as a spiritual lesson for us. Names of persons, places, animals, seas, rivers, cities and mountains are pregnant with meaning. The first bride and mother in all the world was named Adam and it was not until AFTER the fall that she was named Eve, which means "the Mother of the Living One." Here is a marvelous Spirit-inspired prophecy. Four thousand years before Christ was born Adam saw that his wife was to become the Mother of the Living One and thus, he changed her name to Eve. Abram had his name changed to Abraham and Sarai's name was changed to Sarah. In each case the letter "H" was added to their name. The word Abram means "high Father," while the word Abraham means "the Father of a multitude," and thus Abram lost the *high* from his name. The word Sarai means "My princess," while the word Sarah means simply "princess." Thus Sarah lost the "My" and the little "i." Abram lost the big HIGH and Sarah lost the little i and thus the change of name signifies a change in nature. Jacob's name was changed to Israel. The word Jacob means "supplanter, rascal or cheater." The word Israel means "Prince with God," and thus Jacob lost his rascality and became God's prince. It is just the same today. God will take the tall *High* out of us and He will take the little *i* out of us if He gets even half a chance. God will take the rascality out of us and we shall become God's princes. Saul of Tarsus had his name changed to Paul. The word Saul means *big* and the word Paul means *little* and hence the BIG was knocked out of Paul just as the HIGH was knocked out of Abram and the Rascality was knocked out of Jacob. This is sufficient to prove that there is a profound meaning to all Bible names.

The names of the twelve sons of Jacob set forth the plan of salvation from start to finish. Jacob may not have realized it, but whatsoever things were written aforetime were written for our learning.

REUBEN

Reuben was the first born of Jacob, the beginning of his strength, the excellency of dignity and the excellency of power and might. The word Reuben means *behold a son.* When the boy was born the happy Mother was sure the Lord had looked upon her affliction. His name was called Reuben. This is exactly what takes place whenever a person repents of his sins and believes on the Lord Jesus Christ to the saving of the soul; BEHOLD A SON. Regeneration makes us a member of the royal order of Reubenites.

SIMEON

Simeon was the second son of Jacob. The word Simeon means to hearken. The word hearken is a combination of two words which means to hear and understand. The Mother of Simeon was satisfied that the Lord had *heard* the cry of her heart and *understood* her sorrow. She named her boy Simeon because the Lord had heard that she was hated. God had, therefore, given her this son and his name was called Simeon. Exactly so. After we are born of the

Spirit of God, the Lord hears and understands our every need. We hearken to God and He hears the cry of His children and knoweth their sorrows. Let us learn to listen to God and He will listen to us. The third son was called Levi.

LEVI

Levi means joined. When he was born the Mother was sure that her husband would now be joined unto her and therefore his name was called Levi. After we are born again and while we listen to God hearkening to the voice of His word, we become conscious of our oneness with Him. We are joined to the Lord and joined to all the Lord's people. We are one with God and one with the people of God.

JUDAH

Judah was the fourth son of Jacob. The word Judah means praise. At his birth the mother had a joy spell and praised God aloud. After we are born again we begin a life of praise. One of the great secrets of a robust, healthy, vigorous Christian life is to learn to praise God. The baseball crowd believes in shouting, the political hosts believe in shouting, and we ought to shout the praises of God. We need some sermons on praise as well as on prayer. Praise will put wings on our prayers. What do you say if we join *the royal order of praisers*. What do you say if we stop our grumbling and growling and complaining and criticizing and murmuring and slandering and back-biting and begin to shout the praises of God. Let us join the tribe of Judah.

ZEBULUN

Zebulun is the name of the fifth son mentioned in Genesis 49 and the word Zebulun means *to dwell or to abide*. When he was born the delighted Mother was satisfied that her husband would dwell with her and his name was called Zebulun. After we are savingly converted to God (Reuben) and while listening to God (Simeon) and continuing to praise God (Judah), we shall soon discover it to be our high privilege to be sanctified wholly and thus enjoy the abiding blessing (Zebulun). We shall dwell in the secret place of the most high and abide under the shadow of the Almighty. Let us become members of the ancient order of R. S. J. Z. Amen.

ISSACHAR

Issachar means *to serve or to be hired*. At his birth the happy Mother realized that God had given her the desire of her heart and she called his name Issachar. After being saved and sanctified we should all join the tribe of Issachar and serve. God has no lazy people. All God's people are hired. After we are converted (Reuben) and filled with the Spirit (Zebulun) and begin to live a life of Praise (Judah), then we commence to work; we begin to serve. If we cannot be a leader and pull, we may get behind and push. Bench warmers are brakes. Let us join the tribe of Issachar and attempt something for God before we die.

DAN

Dan means *to judge*. When he was born the

mother said that God had judged her, therefore, called his name Dan. If we keep true to God we shall judge the world and not only judge the world, but judge angels. In the meantime we are to judge ourselves for if we judge ourselves the Lord will not judge us. Do not judge others. We are living in a day of mercy and not judgment. If we must judge at all let us judge ourselves.

GAD

Gad was the next boy born into the home and Gad means *to overcome.*

The idea intended to be conveyed is that God was equal to an army of soldiers, for one shall chase a thousand and two shall put ten thousand to flight. Shamgar slew an army with an ox goad. David defeated the Philistines with a sling and stone. The uplifted hands of Moses put to confusion the Amalekites. God has ordained that we should be overcomers. The seven churches of Revelation are given to overcomers. There is no excuse for weakness or defeat.

ASHER

Asher means *to be happy.* Happiness was the exultant note at his birth. The Christian life is a happy life. The Christian religion is a happy religion. Christ is the great "happifier."

NAPHTALI

Naphtali means *to wrestle.* When he was born the happy mother said "With great wrestlings have I wrestled and have prevailed" and his name was called Naphtali. We wrestle not against flesh and blood.

JOSEPH

Joseph means *to increase or to add*. Joseph was to be a fruitful bow by a well. We, too, are commanded to add to our faith, virtue and to virtue, knowledge and kindness, and to grow in grace and to increase in the knowledge of God. Have we more love and more fire and more power and more joy and more glory than we had in our yesterdays? If not, there is something wrong with us.

BENJAMIN

The last name on the list is Benjamin. His name was Benoni, which means *son of sorrow*. His name was changed to Benjamin, which means *son of my right hand*. The son of sorrow thus became the son of the Father's right hand. After we are born again, after we are sanctified wholly, and while we watch and pray and walk in the light, we shall pass from this world of sorrow and become seated at the Father's right hand. Here is salvation from start to finish. Not only so, but Christ was the true son (Reuben). He heard and understood the Word and Will of God (Simeon). He was one with the Father (Levi). His holy life was a sweet smelling incense (Judah). He dwelt in the secret place of the most high (Zebulun), and was the servant of God and the servant of man (Issachar) and is now the judge of all the earth

(Dan). He was the Conqueror of sin and Satan
(Gad), was the one who would yield royal
dainties (Asher). He is the true vine (Joseph)
and of the increase of His government and
peace there shall be no end. He was the Son
of Sorrow (Benoni), but now has a new name
and is the Son of the Father's right hand (Benjamin).

GENESIS AND CHRIST

The book of Genesis is Christo-Centric. Every chapter centers in the Christ of God. Adam was a fore-
shadowing of Christ as God's perfect man, reigning, rul-
ing over a sinless creation. The seed of the woman was
a foreshadowing of the virgin birth of God. Abel suffering innocently and dying because he was more righteous than his brother was a type of Christ as the innocent sufferer, suffering because he was more righteous than His brother. Abel's lamb pointed to the
Lamb of God, which taketh away the sin of the world.
Noah, the preacher of righteousness, the just and righteous and perfect man, living in obedience to the Divine
Will was a type of Christ as the preacher of righteousness, fulfilling in even minute details the plans and purposes of God. The ark was also a foreshadowing of
Christ as the only place of safety, security and enjoyment. It pointed unerringly to Christ, our ark, as the
only place of safety and salvation for us. Isaac, the loving son of the obedient father submitting himself to his
father's will pointed forward to Christ as the obedient
Son of a loving Father, God. Joseph, suffering innocently and exalted to a throne and saving the world from
perishing, was a foreshadowing of the Greater than
Joseph, who was misrepresented, maligned, misjudged

and suffering innocently, is now exalted to a throne of grace and glory and finally will save the world from perishing. Melchisedek, the priest of the most high God, without father or mother or beginning of days or end of life, pointed forward to our great high priest, Jesus Christ, the priest and king of Peace even the one who now liveth to make intercession for us.

The ten names of Genesis, beginning with Adam and ending with Noah, portray our Lord Jesus Christ as the substitute, dying, rising again, pouring out the Holy Ghost, and the coming King, who will usher in the millennial rest.

The twelve names of Genesis 49, beginning with Reuben and ending with Benjamin, foreshadow the Son of God, who was one with God and as the "Man of sorrows and acquainted with grief" became our Benjamin, the son of the Father's right hand. Isaac's ram offered up instead of Isaac foreshadowed the great consecrated substitute, our ram, Jesus Christ, who died that we might live. The tree of life in the midst of the Paradise of God, in the Garden of Eden, pointed to Christ as the tree of life, who even now is in the midst of the Paradise of God. The angel of the Lord mentioned many times in Genesis, was undoubtedly a personal manifestation of the pre-incarnate Christ. It was Christ who created the heavens and the earth. It was Christ who shut out Adam and Eve after they had sinned. It was Christ who visited with Abraham under the tree. It was Christ who wrestled with Jacob and conquered him. The angel of the Lord in the Old Testament was the Christ of the New Testament. The water of Life sets forth Christ as the water of life. The Shiloh of Genesis 49 is the Christ of Matthew. An Outline of Genesis in Seven Words.

Adam
Abel
Noah
Abraham
Isaac
Jacob
Joseph

Eight Great historic events present the Book of Genesis
in a nutshell.
Creation
Fall
Flood
Babel
Abraham's Call
Isaac's Bride
Jacob's Flight
Joseph's Escape

All the great doctrines are found in Genesis
1. Creation.
"In the beginning God created"
2. Salvation by Blood.
a. Coats of Skins
b. Abel's Lamb
c. Abraham's Heifer
3. Substitution.
a. Seth instead of Abel
b. Isaac's Ram
4. Justification.
a. Abraham when 75 years of age
b. Jacob at Bethel
5. Sanctification.
a. Abraham when 99 years of age
b. Jacob at Peniel

6. Retribution.
    a. Flood
    b. Sodom
7. Election.
    a. Isaac instead of Ishmael
    b. Jacob instead of Esau

Genesis answers the burning questions of the day.

1. Whence came matter?
    "In the beginning God created."

2. Whence came man?
    "And the Lord God formed man."

3. Whence came sin?
    "The earth was without form and void."
    "Because . . ." Genesis 3:17.

4. How to get back to God.
    Coats of Skins
    Abel's lamb

5. How to please God.
    Enoch . . . Abraham

6. How to prevail with God.
    Jacob's Surrender

7. How to win.
    Joseph

The following are a few of the important types in Genesis:

1. Adam, a type of Christ, as being head of the Human race.
2. Enoch, being translated before the flood a type of the bride of Christ.
3. Noah, a type of the Jewish church called to go through the tribulation.
4. Abraham, the typical believer.

5. Melchisedek, a king and priest.
6. Isaac, son and heir, sacrificed.
7. Jacob, the typical Servant just as Isaac was the typical Son and Joseph was the typical Ruler.
8. Joseph, sold by his brethren.
9. Judah, as substitute and surety.
10. Rebekah, Isaac's wife, a type of the bride of Christ.
11. Sarah, a type of the Jews.
12. Rachel, a type of the Bride of Christ, obtained last, but loved best.
13. Eliezer, Abraham's servant, type of the Holy Spirit.
14. Lot, the worldly Christian.

Other types are:

Abel, the righteous, innocent, suffering one.
Abel's Lamb.
Noah's Ark.
The Seed of the woman, of Abraham, of Isaac, and of Jacob.
The offering up of Isaac.
The ladder of Jacob.
The Sufferings and glory of Joseph.

GENESIS FINDS ITS COMPLEMENT IN THE APOCALYPSE

1. Genesis, the book of the beginning. Revelation, the book of the end.
2. The earth created. The earth passed away.
3. Satan's first rebellion. Satan's final rebellion.
4. Sun, moon and stars for earth's government. Sun, moon and stars connected with earth's judgment.
5. Sun to govern the day. No need of the sun.
6. Darkness called night. "No night there."

7. Waters called seas. "No more sea."
8. A river for earth's blessings. A river for the New Earth.
9. Man in God's image. Man again in God's image.
10. Entrance of sin. Development and end of sin.
11. Curse pronounced. "No more curse."
12. Death entered in. "No more death."
13. Cherubim first mentioned in connection with man. Cherubim finally mentioned in connection with man.
14. Man driven out from Eden. Man restored.
15. Tree of life guarded. "Right to the tree of life."
16. Sorrow and suffering enter. No more sorrow.
17. Man's religion, art and science resorted to for enjoyment apart from God. Man's religion, luxury, art and science, judged and destroyed by God.
18. Nimrod, a great rebel and king, and hidden anti-God the founder of Babylon. The Beast a great rebel and king and manifested anti-God, the reviver of Babylon.
19. A flood from God to destroy an evil generation. A flood from Satan to destroy an elect generation.
20. The Bow, the token of God's covenant with the Earth. The Bow, betokening God's remembrance of His covenant.
21. Sodom and Egypt, the place of corruption and temptation. Sodom and Egypt again (spiritually representing Jerusalem).
22. A confederacy against Abraham's people overthrown. A confederacy against Abraham's seed overthrown.
23. Marriage of first Adam. Marriage of last Adam.
24. A bride sought for Abraham's son. A Bride made ready and brought to God's Son.

25. Two angels acting for God on behalf of His people. Two witnesses acting for God on behalf of His people.
26. A promised seed to possess the gate of his enemies. The promised seed coming into Possession.
27. Man's dominion ceased and Satan's begun. Satan's dominion ended and man's restored.
28. The old serpent causing sin, suffering and death. The old serpent bound for 1000 years.
29. The doom of the old serpent pronounced. The doom of the old serpent executed.
30. Sun, moon and stars associated with Israel. Sun, moon and stars again associated with Israel.
31. Paradise Lost. Paradise restored.